CREDIT ANALYSIS 102

What they don't teach you in credit training programs…
A five-part foundation for a successful financial services career

D. NEIL BERDIEV

Published by D. Neil Berdiev, DNB Associates, Boston, MA

First edition, March 2012
ISBN: 0977411710
ISBN 13: 9780977411719

Library of Congress Control Number: 2012907989
DNB Associates, Boston, MA

TABLE OF CONTENTS

ACKNOWLEDGEMENTS vii

INTRODUCTION – TRAINING VACUUM AND LACK OF THE
NEXT LEVEL SKILL SET. xi

THE QUOTE xvii

PART I - BEYOND NUMBER CRUNCHING 1

    CHAPTER I – NUMBERS ARE ONLY A FRACTION OF SUCCESS, A SMALL ONE TOO 3

    CHAPTER II – THE ANALYST'S SUCCESS PIE 9

    CHAPTER III – THE PROGRESSION OF SKILL BUILDING 15

    CHAPTER IV – ONE STEP AT TIME, BUT AT YOUR OWN PACE 21

    CHAPTER V – BUILDING ON YOUR STRENGTHS VERSUS ELIMINATING
    YOUR WEAKNESSES AND EVERYTHING ELSE IN BETWEEN 25

    CHAPTER VI – THINKING ONE STEP AHEAD, ACTING ONE STEP AHEAD 29

    CHAPTER VII – LEARNING FROM THE BEST – THE ANALYST'S CREED 35

PART II – BUILDING A REPUTATION – YOU REAP WHAT YOU SOW.....37

    CHAPTER I – IT TAKES A LIFETIME TO BUILD AND A DAY TO LOSE 39

    CHAPTER II – KNOW WHAT THE EXPECTATIONS ARE BEFORE YOU CHANGE THE
    WORLD 47

CHAPTER III – PERCEPTION IS NOT EVERYTHING, BUT... 53

CHAPTER IV – THE VARIOUS "INTEREST GROUPS" – MULTI-TIER AUDIENCES TO PLEASE 59

CHAPTER V – YOU CAN'T BE KNOWN FOR EVERYTHING...............................65

CHAPTER VI – LEARNING FROM THE BEST – LESSONS FROM A BANKING EXECUTIVE 71

PART III – FIND YOUR PLACE ON THE PLANE..75

CHAPTER I – BETWEEN MEDIOCRITY AND EXCELLENCE – THERE IS A PLACE FOR EVERYBODY 77

CHAPTER II – JOB VERSUS CAREER PATH 83

CHAPTER III – THE NEW GENERATION OF BANKERS. ARE WE READY? 89

CHAPTER IV – ARE YOU WILLING TO PUT IN AN EFFORT TO EARN YOUR PLACE? 95

CHAPTER V – BE SMART, KNOW YOUR OPTIONS AND HAVE A STRATEGY, A LONG-TERM ONE 101

CHAPTER VI – YOUR NETWORK IS YOUR GROWTH FUEL..........................105

CHAPTER VII – LEARNING FROM THE BEST – ONLINE NETWORKING ESSENTIALS FOR THE 21ST CENTURY 111

PART IV – HOW BADLY DO YOU WANT IT? 115

CHAPTER I – THE SKY'S THE LIMIT BUT BEING REALISTIC DOES NOT HURT 117

CHAPTER II – CREATING YOUR OWN OPPORTUNITIES 123

CHAPTER III – GOING ABOVE AND GOING BEYOND....................................129

CHAPTER IV – FORGET WHAT THEY TOLD YOU – THEY LIED! 135

CHAPTER V – PATIENCE IS SOMETHING THEY JUST DON'T TEACH YOU 139

CHAPTER VI – LEARNING FROM THE BEST – LESSONS FROM A BANKING CEO.......145

PART V – GETTING IT DONE IS THE NAME OF THE GAME
(PERIOD!)...149

CHAPTER I – IS YOUR GLASS HALF FULL OR HALF EMPTY? 151

CHAPTER II – RESULTS ORIENTATION – EFFORT IS GREAT BUT IT DOESN'T
LAST FOREVER 159

CHAPTER III - WHAT DO YOU WANT TO BE KNOWN FOR AND HOW WILL IT
TRANSLATE INTO OPPORTUNITIES? 165

CHAPTER IV – GET IT DONE AND FIX IT LATER 171

CHAPTER V – NO ONE CARES ABOUT WHAT YOU WANT, UNLESS … 177

CHAPTER VI – LEARNING FROM THE BEST – LESSONS FROM A BANKING CEO.......181

THE PREVIEW FOR CREDIT ANALYSIS 103 183

AFTERWORD 189

ACKNOWLEDGEMENTS

A number of people helped me create this book and I would like to express my appreciation for their assistance, inspiration and invaluable input.

This book has been inspired in part and shaped by the work of Ginny O'Brien. I first came across her book *Coaching Yourself to Leadership* a couple of years ago. It was written well and wrapped the strategy of becoming a quality coaching leader into simple to follow and execute terms. This is when I began thinking of qualities that make an outstanding credit analyst. The resulting product is the five point strategy in front of you.

As this writing endeavor progressed, I have talked to many individuals who provided me with their thoughts, ideas and helped further shape the direction for my book. These individuals include my fellow lending and credit colleagues at Boston Private Bank as well as other institutions in New England and beyond, my fellow board members of the RMA New England Chapter, my former banking colleagues and others in the financial services community. I have also benefited from the input of individuals outside of the world of finance, including training and development executives such as Richard Spada of Novartis and Bruce Green of Boston Scientific (now retired). Last but not least, I sought advice of education professionals, including David Green who works in the MA public schools system and Professor James Hunt of Babson College.

I would also like to acknowledge the assistance of Jackye Pope who was the book editor. This was the second opportunity I have had to work with her. I have come to appreciate her style that fixes my writing of a non-native English speaker, yet preserves my personal style and approach to writing.

Since I wrote my first book in 2005-2006, the publishing market has continued to become more competitive, transparent, cost-effective, and efficient. I continue to be the publisher of my books but there are companies and individuals who make various components of the publishing process happen. So, thank you for doing what you are doing.

To Dina, Chapa and Tauri

For even on the worst day always managing to put a smile on my face

INTRODUCTION – TRAINING VACUUM AND LACK OF THE NEXT LEVEL SKILL SET

The story of Credit Analysis 102 started over a decade ago when I entered the commercial banking industry. At that time the industry appeared to offer a path to a very promising career. However, it took just a few months to realize something any industry insider knows painfully well – good training is an endangered and in many organizations it is an extinct species. About 15 years later, I continue to observe that the reality of training in banking has not changed; in fact, it has even deteriorated. The thorough and comprehensive training programs that were around for many years are a bittersweet memory. The same can be said about the coaching skills of managers and the quality of management training and mentoring programs. Trends and indicators keep pointing to the fact that banks invest less and less in training. Training quality and comprehensiveness is gone, and real training know-how is being lost.

What we are left with is generations of up-and-coming commercial bankers who lack the most essential skills, and are therefore precluded from having accomplished and fulfilling careers. What turns this problem into an impending crisis is the fact that the industry is gradually losing the trained and experienced generations that are nearing retirement. In the meantime, the younger generations slated to replace them do not have proper training and experience to lead the way. Since the world economy is facing at least a myopic, multi-year recovery as this book is being written, it is reasonable to conclude that investment in training is not likely to pick up. As a result, the challenge of finding qualified employees is poised to get worse and worse in the coming years. If the economy improves, the challenge is even greater, as competition for high-quality employees is likely to intensify.

Just as my bank and my team are now struggling to find qualified candidates with some credit background and experience, our competitors consistently cite similar challenges. It is also personally frustrating to see a very high pile of resumes from inexperienced yet capable candidates who would love to have a chance to get into the industry yet find that doors are closed to them due to the lack of training. Almost no banks are able to provide a comprehensive training platform for these individuals to develop and thrive. Some provide informal training but those programs lack structure and their quality varies widely and is often only as good as the individual managers who deliver them. And imagine the possibilities – generations of bankers will be entering decision-making roles without the proper credit foundation for making sound lending decisions. I wonder if the so-called Great Recession of 2008-2009 will seem like a slight economic hiccup compared to what lies ahead.

So, when did training become an afterthought, and the area that loses budgets as one of the first courses of action when banks need to manage earnings (by managing costs)? When did it become a cost center, with little value attached, and the element most likely to be cut at the first opportunity? When did maximizing employee value begin to be associated with piling more work on them, while ignoring the fact that they need training to be more effective and to help them in their careers' progression?

Perhaps it is just the continuation of the short-term focus of executive teams that survive from one quarterly earnings report to another without a sustainable long-term strategy. Possibly, it is also a reflection of how little importance we place on investment in human capital and on developing and retaining talent. We expect that our borrowers will continuously invest in long-term capital assets that will provide the foundation for successful performance in the future. Naturally, fixed assets are one type of long-term capital asset. Smart organizations understood years ago that human capital is another capital asset that needs ongoing investment. Yet, we as banks do not practice what we preach.

While writing this book, I interviewed a number of bankers across the country. They provided valuable feedback that offered further context for the issue:

- Diverse formal (and less formal) credit training existed in the 1970s-1980s at larger and in some instances at smaller organizations. These programs included many months of classroom sessions followed by several on-the-job rotations.

- This training began to deteriorate due to shrinking budgets in the 1980s-1990s (largely in the 1990s) and onward. In some instances the decrease in training was due to acquisitions by larger banks that paid less attention to the regions they were acquiring. The balance shifted to sales while credit / credit training became a secondary or even lesser priority. Another cause cited is the growing reliance on credit scoring methodologies.

- Several respondents saw increasing turnover among employees as a cause of less training (although in my opinion it is a poor excuse for any organization's inability to attract, develop and retain talent).

- Credit training is one of the first budgets to get axed in the early phases of a recession. It is easy to cut training as cuts will not lead to immediate negative results but instead have a longer term impact. With bank mergers and an overall focus on quarterly earnings, management teams lost sight of what's important in the long term (investment in human capital).

- In good times banks are less likely to invest in training because there is less to worry about.

- Banks have yet to learn from the recent (on-going) recession. There is a tendency to blame the economy for deteriorating loan portfolios rather than the lack of credit experience that stems from the lack of credit training.

The disappearance of training is only a part of the challenge. When I was going through various credit training programs, I came to the conclusion that each program taught numerous credit skills. However, most if not all of those skills focused on number crunching. The ability to crunch numbers and read ratios accounts for an important but a very small portion of what constitutes an accomplished credit analyst. A big part of credit proficiency and being at the top of this field is based on those numerous non-quantitative skills that some will acquire and others will not. Those who figure out what it takes to become an outstanding credit analyst will do it through a process of trial-and-error (I call it "earn your own bruises") or through coaching and mentoring relationships with more tenured bankers. However, there are many more analysts who will never figure out those skills. Training programs, even in their hey day, were silent on this topic.

Why is it so hard to teach what I would call the 102-level skills? It is much easier to pinpoint and teach quantitative aspects than the more subtle qualitative skills and abilities. There is a lack of appreciation and understanding of those key qualitative factors that will eventually take your proficiency as a credit analyst to an advanced level. You may also observe the lack of understanding on the part of banks that employee development does not stop after the initial credit training effort. We keep hiring and training analysts who may be good with numbers but undoubtedly fall short of developing their full potential and developing into A-level analysts. There are plenty of examples of credit analysts with reasonably good initial credit training who soon reach the ice age of their development and find themselves in a learning vacuum. The result? The banking talent pool contains so much potential, but most of it stays at the "potential" level.

And this is what brings me to this book. After many years of roadblocks on the path of my learning and development, an idea was born to create something that has been missing across the industry – the knowledge tools that will allow credit analysts and other banking and financial services professionals to build more successful careers. It is crafted around five key qualities that, in my opinion, are the very foundation of Credit Analysis 102 – Beyond number crunching; Reputation; Finding your place in the world of credit and banking; Your drive; and Getting it done.

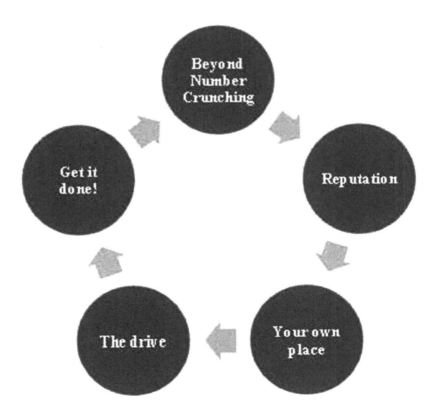

I hope that you will enjoy this book and find it to be a practical, actionable, inspiring and sustaining resource.

D. Neil Berdiev
September 15, 2010

THE QUOTE

This book is about excellence in whatever we do, whether the examples of such excellence happen from time to time or exist as your daily joie de vivre (your life motto or your modus operandi). This is why I would like to open with a quote by Charles R. Swindoll that should serve as an inspiration for you in going above and beyond in your life. When my team looks to hire credit analysts, after the right candidates are selected, this quote is what their orientation program begins with and its guiding principles continue to shape their daily work.

"The longer I live, the more I realize the impact of attitude on life. Attitude, to me, is more important than facts. It is more important than the past, the education, the money, than circumstances, than failure, than successes, than what other people think or say or do. It is more important than appearance, giftedness or skill. It will make or break a company... a church... a home. The remarkable thing is we have a choice everyday regarding the attitude we will embrace for that day. We cannot change our past... we cannot change the fact that people will act in a certain way. We cannot change the inevitable. The only thing we can do is play on the one string we have, and that is our attitude. I am convinced that life is 10% what happens to me and 90% of how I react to it. And so it is with you... we are in charge of our Attitudes."

PART I -

BEYOND NUMBER CRUNCHING

CHAPTER I –
NUMBERS ARE ONLY A FRACTION OF SUCCESS, A SMALL ONE TOO

Even the impressive Amazon forests for all their might and irreplaceable value are built out of small building blocks of soil, plants and other living tissue. There is an endless list of components that go into creating the Amazon and the disappearance of one tiny element can make the entire forests disappear.

Quotes without an attribution are my own ramblings...

Every financial or credit analyst training program begins with the fundamentals of teaching entry-level analysts how to read, understand and then interpret financial statements correctly, quickly and effectively. A larger part of any comprehensive credit training program is focused on Commercial and Industrial (C&I) Lending (as opposed to Commercial Real Estate (CRE) Lending). C&I lending is focused on lending to non-real estate operating companies ranging from small mom-and-pop shops with basic tax returns to publicly traded multinational corporations with dozens of pages of audited financial statements. Knowledge of financial accounting and, to some extent, managerial accounting is the rudimentary skill set of every credit analyst who analyzes C&I credits. Without this knowledge, a person will never become a real analyst, whether we are talking about investment or commercial banking or other financial fields. In addition, a knowledge of accounting is usually a prerequisite to getting a job as a credit analyst at any established, mid- to large-size bank or financing firm as well as at an increasing number of smaller banks. This is Credit 101.

Here are some number crunching basics you must have in your arsenal if you want to become a successful credit analyst. You must be able to:

- Read and understand a wide range of financial statements

- Prepare financial statement spreads with high levels of accuracy

- Break down these financial statements and reassemble them in the format required for proper analysis

- Run calculations correctly, including but not limited to cash flows

- Ask relevant questions to understand what's behind the numbers

- Interpret correctly the trends in front of you with a focus on understanding the most relevant risks

Again, without a solid knowledge of accounting and of financial statements, you will never become a high-caliber analyst; potentially you might not have the chance to become an analyst at all. Once you have succeeded in this very first challenge of becoming a credit analyst, there is a major risk. The knowledge of numbers can be empowering, and not in a good way. One story to share is the story of Alex, who was an aspiring analyst during his undergraduate years at a New England college (his identity, and the identity of other examples used in this book were changed, but the essence of these real-life stories was not). Alex was very bright and driven. He thoroughly researched what the main requirements for securing a job as a credit analyst at a good sized, reputable bank would be. The message from his mentors as well as his professors was consistent – good accounting knowledge and strong writing skills were must-haves if he wanted to out-compete the other candidates.

Armed with this knowledge, Alex focused on majoring in accounting. He also took writing classes and developed the necessary writing proficiencies. Alex's hiring managers were impressed with his ability to understand the income statement and the balance sheet, and how they converge and reconcile in the statement of cash flows. They were further impressed to see that Alex aced some of the more technical topics related to different inventory accounting methods, accounting for retirement liabilities, and several others. His solid writing skills were recognized as an asset and as something not even every tenured employee possessed. As a reward for his focused preliminary work, Alex fairly easily secured a job as an entry-level analyst at a superregional bank in Boston upon graduating from college.

Within a month of starting his job, Alex was signed up for a rigorous Loan Officer Development Program and completed it at the top of his class. Upon his successful graduation from the program, Alex began to feel that he was prepared to move to the next level – structuring and underwriting debt financing deals. In many instances he clearly saw that his ability to understand financial statements and crunch numbers was by far superior of that of his more senior colleagues. However, he was left to do statement spreads, industry research and a number of other less than glamorous tasks that he regarded as administrative. He developed a negative attitude, which adversely affected relationships with his colleagues to the point that management began having reservations about Alex's ability to grow and advance as an analyst. Seeing potential in Alex and wanting to give him one more chance, his team leader agreed to let him underwrite one deal to showcase his skills. Alex was excited about the opportunity and was determined to demonstrate his skills to everyone. To his dismay, after a week of long hours of work he reached a state of what could only be described as analysis-paralysis.

What Alex discovered very quickly is that even with his strong knowledge of accounting, there are many other competencies and skills that need to be developed to become a seasoned analyst. Many can only be developed by practicing the trade and reinforcing what is learned in the classroom. One major expertise is the ability to integrate financial analysis into a deal structure, to be able to properly mitigate risks, to learn to see the big picture and to incorporate the details of analysis into a cohesive presentation. One more curve ball was the fact that once it was his signature authority on the line (i.e. his name, reputation and responsibility for a potentially poor decision), he kept on analyzing, analyzing, and analyzing the deal and did not know when enough was enough. What he lacked, among various factors and experience, is the confidence of having underwritten and structured dozens, if not hundreds, of deals.

The mistakes Alex made are very common, from rookies to mid-level analysts. Knowledge of accounting and how to read financial statements can provide a misguided sense of confidence that you are ready to enter the major leagues; in some cases I have seen during my career there is even a sense of cockiness and arrogance on the part of recent credit training graduates who know numbers and numbers only. This is why there is something to be said about the actual experience of working on deal after deal to be able to fuse the numerous elements and components that go into putting together a solid debt financing transaction.

As for Alex, he learned his lesson the hard way. Luckily for him, his team and team manager were forgiving, and he was smart enough to acknowledge and learn from his mistakes. The last time I was in contact with Alex, he had become a very successful commercial lending team leader at a national bank, still deeply rooted in the credit fundamentals he learned many years ago.

One way to overcome the false sense of confidence that a knowledge of financial statement analysis can give you is by staying humble and realizing that you are in the very early stages of your career. Of course, this is easier said than done, and the temptation to do otherwise is often strong. As William Gurnall eloquently stated, "humility is a necessary veil to all other graces." Always remember that you truly know nothing and that you have a very long way to go before you do, and that you will never know everything. Some of the most successful bankers and non-bankers will tell you that this is the best attitude to have no matter how high you climb in your career. If you conquer this challenge, your chances of joining the ranks of top-notch credit analysts will rise dramatically.

CHAPTER II – THE ANALYST'S SUCCESS PIE

As I go through my career and through my life, the more I learn, the more I realize how little I know and how much more there is to learn and discover. I wonder if this will ever change. I sure hope not….

Many years ago I had a mentor who asked me who I was professionally. Naturally, my answer was that I was a credit analyst. He responded that this was one way to look at things – a very narrow, tunnel-like way. When I asked what other ways there were, his response was that I should look at myself as a person in possession of a set of transferable skills. Those skills are the skills every one of us acquires, augments, and polishes day after day and year after year. It did not quite sink in and resonate with me until many years later, but I keep coming back to that conversation, especially as I now manage a team of analysts, helping them develop into high-caliber credit and lending professionals.

Here is how the concept works. You can see yourself as a credit analyst, working at XYZ commercial bank, based in MA and servicing a narrow range of customers. All anyone else hears is "blah, blah, blah…." Do you know how many thousands of credit analysts working at commercial banks there are? That is hardly appealing to every employer. It feels quite average and mediocre. Another way to look at yourself and your career is in terms of pursuing a path that allows you to develop a variety of transferrable qualities. I would compare it to a software program that undergoes an evolution, from the very basic 1.0 version to a much more complex and expanded 2.0, 3.0, and other more sophisticated versions of its original self. Here is an example description of the qualities of an advanced level credit analyst:

I am:

- An experienced financial analyst with the ability to analyze a broad range of corporate and personal financial statements;

- An analyst who has underwritten hundreds of deals to borrowers in a (long) list of industries;

- An analyst who has participated in structuring hundreds of deals that included structured finance, asset-based lending facilities, private equity and venture capital financing, and many others;

- An analyst who has managed on average 5 to 6 deals at a time and has underwritten on average 120 to 140 deals (full underwriting!) annually, in addition to other analyst responsibilities;

- An analyst who has strong writing skills;

- An analyst who has managed deals under very tight deadlines and consistently met deadlines and met and exceeded other expectations by working whatever hours were needed to get the job done;

- An analyst who has successfully supported the most experienced, hard-to-work-with and demanding lenders with the most complex loan portfolios.

The above list of examples could go on, but I hope that you begin to see the bigger picture. Analysts and most other professionals are hired because they possess high-quality, transferrable skills. Those who do not succeed in developing an important range of transferrable qualities usually fall behind and do not develop and grow as well as others. In some instances, they may be fired because they lack those essential skills. As the previous chapter discussed, the ability to understand and interpret financial statements is the skill that falls into the realm of number crunching skills. It is the most rudimentary skill in your tool box but without it you will not succeed as a credit analyst. There are, however, numerous other qualities you will need to develop if you would like to excel in the field of commercial credit and lending. The chart that follows will help outline those skills.

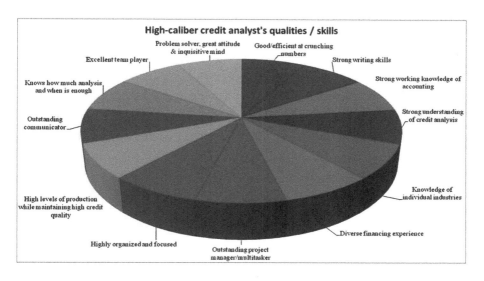

Many of these skills are developed over time and are built on the foundation of other, more basic ones. The majority of them continue to be enhanced during your entire career. As your career progresses, it is essential to continue learning by working on hundreds of financing opportunities in order to understand how they are being structured and why. Another, higher level skill involves the financing of companies in a wide range of industries. I would recommend that a less-experienced analyst be a generalist to expose himself or herself to as many financing opportunities as possible. Also do not forget that these experiences cannot be learned in the classroom or during theoretical discussions. There are so many nuances to real-life scenarios that can only be appreciated over the course of months and years of financing.

One true crown jewel of any credit analyst is the ability to pick up a new deal, ask a few relevant questions, and in a matter of minutes have a high level understanding of what the deal is all about, what the key risks are and what the strategy for underwriting should be. When you have this particular skill, you may confidently conclude that your Credit Analysis 102 Diploma has been earned.

While it may seem that some pie slices in the chart above are bigger than others, they should not be interpreted as being of greater importance than others. I have always stayed away from assigning weights to specific qualities. What's more important is to realize that the chart represents a wide range of qualities you are yet to develop. It is just as valuable to have a full appreciation for what it means to be a well-rounded credit analyst possessing a broad range of skills. An emphasis on some qualities over others and the fine balance among all of them will depend on your personal strengths and weaknesses, your organization and its needs, your career goals, the state of the economy, and a slew of other factors.

I recall a story from very early in my career. I worked with an analyst we'll call Jonathan. Jonathan, or Jon, was catching new information on the fly, and I always envied his natural ability to grasp quickly what our trade is all about. After a number of months of working with Jon, I began to notice his obsession with financial analysis. He very quickly surpassed all of us on the team in his ability to quickly spread financial statements, correctly calculate the most complex cash flow, collateral and other measures, and deliver a concise and focused analysis outlining all of the key risks. This was however the extent of his success. He was always awkward in dealing with people, especially in managing the conflicts that are common in the work environment. He also had difficulty extracting information from lenders and that information was vital to presenting a well-balanced write-up as opposed to "elevator analysis." Jon was focused more on numbers than on people, and a high performing credit analyst must do both. He had little interest in working on various financing deals and was focused strictly on one particular corner of C&I lending. Jon even told me several times that his competitive edge was in his ability to analyze any financial statement and do it quickly and correctly. He further admitted that other skills were not as important to him. As his fellow analysts began to progress and move up into other opportunities within the organization and beyond, Jon became more and more frustrated. He knew that he was the best when it came to quantitative financial or credit analyses. Yet, his less-experienced team members were becoming portfolio managers and taking other jobs he had hoped to do some day.

One day he summoned his courage and confronted his team leader. The response was a shocking revelation to Jon. His team leader told him that he was just not ready for that next level. When pressed for specifics and explanations, the team leader continued to say that Jon was not mature enough; did not see the importance of helping the team achieve its goals; could not work collaboratively with his fellow co-workers; had not improved his writing skills as suggested; did not handle criticism well; was focused on analysis at the expense of meeting production goals - the list went on and on.

Jon took this feedback very hard and was practically devastated. The list was a lot to handle. Wouldn't you be shocked if all you had previously heard was praise without even an ounce of constructive criticism? It certainly did not help that Jon's team leader did not spend the time to coach him to overcome his weaknesses, and Jon had no idea of his numerous deficiencies (and this is another big problem with his team leader that we will not discuss here). Soon after that conversation, I got a new job and we fell out of touch over time. He was eventually successful, slowly climbing the corporate ladder. Nonetheless, given how intelligent he was versus the pace of his growth, I assume that he did not agree with the feedback from his superiors or may not have done anything about it.

The lesson here is quite simple - the pie chart above is one of many tools. It should NOT be used exclusively to control or limit your development. It should not be viewed as handcuffs but rather as a spring-board. It is a part of the road map to guide you in the right direction and expand your growth opportunities.

- Firstly, the "pie" has to be well-rounded and balanced.

- Secondly, the best way to utilize it is as part of your long-term development planning, as opposed to fueling unrealistic expectations.

- Thirdly, you should develop a pie chart that works for you and your situation. Be creative!

CHAPTER III – THE PROGRESSION OF SKILL BUILDING

Building a great career is like building a beautiful yet environmentally-balanced house – it starts with the foundation, is built up one brick and system at a time, and, once complete, can shine as a masterpiece for the owners to enjoy.

Just like anything in life, building an outstanding transferrable skill set as a credit analyst is a gradual, step-by-step process that starts with the most basic number crunching elements and over time transitions to more sophisticated planes of deal structuring, team work, project management, problem-resolution, conflict management, and many others. Additionally, each skill in itself starts with the basics and leads to more sophisticated manifestations of self. For example, the analysis of basic corporate tax returns and compiled financial statements is the initial step that eventually develops into an expertise in analyzing complex audited financial statements for publicly traded companies and the highly complicated global cash flows of private equity investors.

Once you have tackled the basic statement analysis and credit underwriting, your learning experiences will be increasingly less quantitative and more focused on people and communication skills as well as on the skills of time management, prioritizing, client interaction, portfolio management, and risk management. This is when you begin putting numbers into context and shift from number crunching into true analysis and problem-solving. An example of a less quantitative skill is working effectively with lenders. Even when some of the respective lender-analyst priorities are different, the ultimate goal is the same:

Extending "good" loans that get repaid in full and on time.

Sounds quite simple, doesn't it? However, it is very hard to sustain year after year in real life or we would all be working at highly successful financial institutions and making a lot of money. Within this particular challenge you as an analyst will be learning how to "handle" more tenured and experienced colleagues in a way that gets your job done (for their benefit) very quickly, yet makes them feel that they are in charge, and working toward multiple and tight timelines without "overheating." This is when you will begin realizing that one size does not fit all. The most common challenge for junior analysts is lenders not helping them (i.e. analysts) get the job done – underwriting quickly and efficiently, yet with a high quality of analysis and ensuring that key questions, issues and risks are covered. The less experienced or less successful analysts complain and play the blame game, pointing fingers at the other side. The successful pros do not complain, have a positive attitude when dealing with adversity, take responsibility for their own actions and get the job done no matter what the circumstances are. This is the progression of an analyst's development that evolves from number crunching to qualitative skills, from science to the art of credit analysis. This is why during the first days of analysts' orientation on our team we focus on instilling the following into every analyst:

1. Positive attitude (people get hired and fired for attitude)

2. Flexibility and adaptability

3. Constant curiosity, desire to learn and apply that learning

4. Constant desire to improve

5. Getting the job done and exceeding results and expectations

I recall a situation earlier in my career of working with one experienced lender who, shall we say, really lacked the skills necessary for working with people junior to him (or perhaps with colleagues, period). One day he was so upset with the "quality" of my underwriting work (after it had been approved by my own supervisor) that he threw the write up in my face and told me that the quality of my work "sucked." Was I infuriated and insulted by such an outburst? You bet I was. I certainly could have complained to the bank's human resources officer or even confronted him personally to teach him a lesson. This incident occurred during the period when abusive behavior on the part of a senior officer of a bank would not have been tolerated, and the human resources intervention would have been swift and unforgiving. Instead, my intuition told me to sit down and have him walk me through his issues. After I allowed him to vent, it was fairly easy to prove to him that the quality, and even more, the depth of analysis was lacking because he wanted me to do analysis but did not want to provide any assistance in the process. This was the ice-breaker in our relationship. A few months later, I was practically the only analyst with whom that lender wanted to work. After I left the bank, I received emails from him for many months lamenting the fact that I was no longer with the bank and that it was impossible to get anything done to his satisfaction after I left the team.

Your goal should be to continuously elevate and advance your transferrable skills, in and outside of credit. The moment you stop, not only do you no longer build new skills but your existing skills also begin to degrade. *As they say – if you don't use it, you lose it.* Unfortunately, every credit analyst is at risk of this for many reasons. The main reasons are promotions to more senior positions of responsibility without proper training; an organizational culture that actively or passively discourages learning and development; and people's lack of interest in understanding that learning is a never-ending process. As Henry Ford eloquently stated: "Anyone who stops learning is old, whether at twenty or eighty. Anyone who keeps learning stays young. The greatest thing in life is to keep your mind young."

One good example that comes to mind is the story of Eric. Eric was a credit analyst who had very limited credit training or true credit skills. As the bank he worked for was growing rapidly, he soon had an opportunity to become a portfolio manager and a few years later a relationship manager. During these few years of fast growth, his portfolio grew to become one of the largest at the bank. Very soon his primary focus was to put out fires and take care of existing clients without any capacity to do business development. Unfortunately, he never had a chance to improve his credit skills, neither was there a requirement to do so. Similarly, he was not trained to become a good business developer. By default, he became a portfolio manager and not a good one, liking relatively easy hours and the comfort zone of doing an easy, predictable job with a steady paycheck. It was not Eric's goal to learn and develop whether through classroom training or on the job. Similarly, his team leader and the bank in general had very much the same attitude.

In the end, while Eric was an SVP, he had a level of technical knowledge and expertise comparable to that of a junior portfolio manager or a junior lender. It is as if time had frozen for Eric for a good couple of decades. Sadly, even his division executive admitted to me in a private conversation that the bank and his group did not have a strategy for employee development. He further confessed that the bank's growth was happening at the expense of developing lenders like Eric. Lenders who went through a good credit and lending school at other banks were clearly better performers. Eric's portfolio eventually reached such a large level that he was constantly burdened with too much work; he could not keep up with its demands, let alone worry about his professional development. Over time he was turning into a stressed, demoralized, and disorganized Grinch who did not care much about his career, his colleagues or about the bank, and would switch organizations at the first opportunity. Unfortunately, Eric did not have the courage and comfort level to look around and most likely few banks would have wanted him. Imagine that the bank is faced with an unusual situation such as a change of culture with a shift toward business development or gets acquired when the focus will be on lenders with good technical skills in credit, portfolio management, and sales. Will Eric be able to make the cut?

This brings me to one point I always make to my team members – you have to drive your own consistent and gradual development. Your organization, your superiors, your team, and other constituents will not worry about you unless you worry yourself. It is incredibly easy to get bogged down into a daily routine but it is up to you to keep your head above water. When I hear that individuals have "too much work" and therefore have no time for their own development, what I hear is that they do not want to find time. What this tells me as a supervisor is that you do not care enough about your learning and growth. If you do not care about your development, why should anybody else?

Your future is in your own hands and others do not care about it (well, few good managers do but they are a minority). Your supervisors and organization will likely respond favorably to your desire to learn and grow, if you show them that you care about your future and that you appreciate other people's time when they help you reach your career objectives. Just don't forget that you have to be a strong performer before you get a chance to develop.

CHAPTER IV – ONE STEP AT TIME, BUT AT YOUR OWN PACE

Adopt the pace of nature: her secret is patience. Ralph Waldo Emerson

One mistake less-experienced analysts make is trying to learn everything overnight. With driven employees who are yet to accomplish so much, there is a natural hunger to learn, grow, and advance. Unfortunately, we all have seen some inadvertent side effects of overzealousness and a lack of patience. You cram in great deal of information without getting a chance to apply the knowledge and make it part of your readily-available skill arsenal.

What you will discover over the years is that learning can take many forms and shapes:

- Formal classroom;

- Less formal training sessions;

- Coaching session with your boss and others within your organization;

- Learning from your mentors;

- Learning on your own from various sources;

- Learning by doing your job; and, my personal favorite,

- Learning by making mistakes, or as they say learning from your own bumps and bruises.

If you want to learn the smart way, don't earn all of your own bumps and bruises. Instead, learn from other people's mistakes. Some mistakes are certainly fine to make on your own. But if you try to repeat every single mistake that other people made just to learn, very soon your colleagues will question whether you are smart enough for the job. Another important lesson that usually takes time for more junior employees to get is that some of the best learning can happen on the job through a combination of a) applying in real life what you learned in the classroom, and b) by learning as you do the actual job.

Answer the following questions: How many people truly do preparatory work for classes and training sessions they attend? How many people are truly present during all of classroom training or other similar forms of learning? Have you caught yourself focusing on something else during training (such as checking your email) and telling yourself that you will pull out the materials at your leisure and make sure you review them to retain that knowledge? Does the follow-up really happen? Probably not. Lastly, how often do you find yourself in a situation when you have learned great deal, yet you go back to your old ways without implementing at least a couple of the lessons you have learned? I think most if not all of these situations will sound familiar to you.

This is why I am a big believer in:

a) Learning gradually and progressively;

b) Breaking down new information and experiences into smaller components (or chunks) to improve retention; and

c) Ensuring that you put your learning into practice.

You should not assume that the above means it will take a very long time to learn the most basic content. First and foremost determine the pace of learning you are most comfortable with. Be aggressive, yet realistic with your goals. Bob Rivers, the President of Eastern Bank based in Massachusetts, shared his personal career experience at a CEO Series event organized by my Risk Management Association Young Professionals' Group a few years ago and said: "Set aggressive goals. Even if you fall short, you will go farther than you otherwise would. But make sure that your goals can be accomplished." This is how he was able to achieve his goal of becoming a president of a bank at a fairly young age, even though it took him 2 years longer than originally planned.

A word of caution - do not let others determine your learning pace; at a minimum, ensure that you at least have a say in how fast you develop. This is very, very important! When I was a lot more junior in my career, I had a misfortune of having a team leader who dictated my learning page and I had no input on it. He constantly used to say that it took him so long to learn something or reach a certain level, with a hint that his experiences should be the standard for my pace of growth and development. This was how he tried to justify that I did not need to learn as fast I as could and wanted to. This kind of thinking was always disturbing to me as we all have different intellects and different learning capabilities. If I can learn what took someone else 10 years to learn in half the time, why should I be held back? The caveat here is to always ensure that you learn to maneuver within the system without offending the people who may not have gotten a chance to develop at their own pace. This is particularly important if "those people" are decision-makers and can make your development happen on the terms you are happy with. I learned the hard way how to get what I needed without alienating the individuals who had authority and could put a damper on my pace of learning just because they were in a position to do so.

One of the former analysts on my team made just that kind of mistake. This analyst, whom I will call Jared, always welcomed any opportunity to attend formal training. The experience itself gave him a sense he was learning and got him very excited about his job. It was during those moments that he would get motivated to go above and beyond on the job and produce the results that were expected of everybody on the team. Unfortunately, the rest of the time he was lagging in performance and management's feedback to him had a very brief effect. It was very frustrating for me as well as other managers to see such a duality. Lack of consistency and appreciation for learning outside the classroom earned Jared a poor reputation within the organization and within the team. It was also disappointing to see how he had alienated the very same people who were in charge of developing and growing his career.

You are unlikely to find an organization that wants to develop poor performers. What Jared failed to understand is that training and development at one's own pace is a product of top performance on the job. Without that, you can forget about any learning opportunities.

CHAPTER V – BUILDING ON YOUR STRENGTHS VERSUS ELIMINATING YOUR WEAKNESSES AND EVERYTHING ELSE IN BETWEEN

Concentrate your strengths against your competitor's relative weaknesses. Paul Gauguin

Whether you should capitalize on your strengths or work on reducing and eliminating your weaknesses is a lifelong argument. There is quite of bit of written work on this subject. Will you learn and develop faster if you focus on the former or the latter?

In favor of building on strengths

A number of articles I have come across on this topic seem to point in the direction of building on your strengths.

a) A key rationale is that by focusing on your strengths you can develop and grow faster (may be even fastest).

b) Another explanation mentioned is that people are happier when they focus on applying something they already have, and those qualities can generate results here and now.

c) Some believe that your strengths deteriorate while you focus inordinate amounts of effort on improving weaknesses without a guarantee of success. It happens because you are likely to dilute or reduce your strengths by not "exercising" them while expending your energy on improving your weaknesses.

Thus, the proponents of this approach suggest that you should focus on your strengths.

In favor of reducing or eliminating weaknesses

a) Some proponents of reducing or eliminating weaknesses point out that your true passions will not necessarily be in the areas of your strengths. They point out that a number of people have careers that are build on exploiting their strengths and end up doing what does not make them happy.

b) Others note that people who focus on strengths may not have the right skills to grow in the direction needed. They feel that you enhance your strengths with an accompaniment of new skills that are created by turning your weaknesses into strengths.

c) Finally, some believe that weaknesses will likely reduce the effectiveness of your strengths and, in some cases, can undermine your entire strategy of focusing on strengths, rendering it unsuccessful.

If you asked, why can't someone do both, I think you are closer to real life where the majority of issues are not black and white. There has to be the right balance between the two, and the balance will differ from one individual to another. I came across a Harvard Business Review article titled "Stop Overdoing Your Strengths" that discussed strengths potentially becoming liabilities when you overuse or underuse them. This further supports the strategy for the right balance between the two.

It is certainly a reasonable supposition that in the majority of cases capitalizing on your strengths should be easier since you already have them. One important aspect of getting the most out of your strengths is also understanding how to do so. The fact that you want to take advantage of your strong points does not mean that it will happen without any effort. But how can you achieve that balance between playing off your strengths and minimizing your weaknesses? I suggest utilizing the following thought process or rather questioning approach to arrive at the plan that works for you:

-   On one side, create a list of tasks or responsibilities you are currently performing. On the opposite side create a list of tasks or responsibilities you would like to be involved in.

-   Answer whether you love what you do and whether you get a chance to do what you are really passionate about.

-   Create a list of your key strengths and weaknesses.

-   Determine if your passions are aligned with your strengths or whether they are more clustered around your weaknesses.

-   Will your growth be maximized if you exploit your key strengths or by strengthening your weaknesses? Why and how?

-   Will you grow and learn faster by moving one of your key weaknesses into the arsenal of your strengths? Why and how?

-   Which one would you enjoy the most – focusing on your strength(s), reducing or eliminating weakness(es) or some combination of the two? What combination is relevant to your goals?

Once you have gone through this soul searching process, create an action plan that will reflect your conclusions. It is also natural to periodically change the balance based on your personal and professional evolution. When I was just beginning my commercial banking career as a credit analyst, I was all about credit and could not stand the idea of working in sales. A number of years later, through the pursuit of my first entrepreneurial projects, I gradually developed an interest in and later a passion for sales and business development. Now, I can't imagine how I could have gone through my credit career without trying to "marry" credit and sales.

Your search for the right balance between strengths and weaknesses has to be a very holistic process that is not about determining the right or wrong way but the one that looks at the complete picture and all aspects of your professional and personal aspirations at this point in time. This process is about a) weighing your options, b) coming to reasonably justified conclusions, c) developing a road map with specific goals, and d) pursuing those goals.

If you wonder why I recommend this self-exploration through questioning rather than telling that you should do this or that, the answer is very simple. You need to figure out the ultimate path for yourself. No mentor, coach, or career advisor will do this job better than you will. Stay away from those who say they will. Weigh pros and cons, make a conscious decision and work in the direction chosen. You will never know whether the path you did not pick was the wrong one or the right one. Neither will you ever know if the one you did choose was the best possible option. What I do know is that you will be able to look back and say with confidence that you considered your options and opted to do things this particular way. You will know that it was your own choice and only your choice, making you feel that you were and continue to be in charge of your own development.

CHAPTER VI – THINKING ONE STEP AHEAD, ACTING ONE STEP AHEAD

The best way to predict the future is to create it. Peter F. Drucker

Every successful person is successful because he or she is able to see at least one step ahead. As an analyst you should be no exception. While you should work on polishing your expertise in a gradual and consistent fashion (as discussed in the previous chapters), do not forget that the best way to learn is to anticipate your next learning needs and challenges. This approach will help you avoid looking for your next developmental opportunity right when it is time to learn something new. Why? The risk is having completed one step of your development without having the next one lined up. Depending on your goals and development needs, this could delay your learning by at least a few months and might mean you miss on some good developmental opportunities. It also takes time to identify the next targets and begin working toward them. As far as the timing is concerned, you should consider working toward a new developmental goal while you are in the middle to later stages of completing your current goal. This overlap will ensure that you move from acquiring one skill to another without interruptions and at a faster than average pace.

Everything starts with an idea, plan or aspiration. Without them you will have nothing to work toward. The next step is to plan how to achieve your goal. There are several ways you can build your own road map and below is one of many possible paths. The table at the end of this chapter should help organize your thoughts.

- Start by creating an inventory of your skills, so that you know where you stand on day one. Another way to look at this challenge is through identifying your strengths and weaknesses.

- Think of what you would like to do next. Your goals may range from learning how to provide financing to an unfamiliar industry or underwriting a very complex high profile deal to transitioning into a new lending unit, getting promoted to a more senior position, or securing a job with a new organization, if there is no room for growth in your current company.

- Once you have inventoried your current skills and the skills you are yet to develop, you will be able to rank them by level of importance as it applies to your developmental interests.

- Determine which one or two key skill sets you will need to develop in order to qualify for that next step. The next step learning could include a more in-depth knowledge of something you are currently learning. An example of it could be going through the initial training of financing small C&I borrowers and at the next level learning how to analyze and put together complex structured finance or alternative energy deals.

- Now you are ready to write your wish list and the timeline.

The next question to ask yourself is how you will get the experience you need. Look at all of the options at your disposal. While formal training is a good choice, lack of training budgets and training programs can make formal training less accessible and even impossible. However, there are plenty of other alternatives at your disposal. Below are a few suggestions:

- Some of the easiest to reach resources are your colleagues, both senior and junior, as well as your peers. Through this approach you can also signal your career interests to those individuals. This may open new doors for you at a later date, especially if you are highly successful in your current job.

- An extension of the above is working with your team leader in getting you exposed to desired types of learning. You may also ask your manager to help in getting you coaching in a particular area of knowledge. If you are a high performing analyst, you will be surprised how resourceful your team can be in helping you meet your aspirations.

- Self-guided study is a powerful, cost-effective and often underestimated option. This includes training materials that may be available though your employer as well as industry resources through organizations such as the Risk Management Association. The key, as I mentioned previously, is to apply this new knowledge successfully.

- Finding a mentor is also one of those overlooked sources of learning and development.

- Do not forget about working on special projects that not only add value to your organization but also create a learning experience and possibly visibility. It is even more rewarding if you come up with an idea for that special project.

To prevent some frustration on your part, don't forget that some elements of advancement are outside of your control. If you are thinking about becoming a portfolio manager and you are currently an analyst, there are a number of details that will need to line up in order to make your promotion a reality. They include the need of your business units for more portfolio managers, an adequate pool of analyst candidates to replace you, the size and growth rate of your organization, the pool of other analysts competing against you, and many other factors.

Yet, a slew of factors are within your sphere of influence. They can include the quality of your work (not just efforts but results!), the satisfaction of your team leader and the organization with your performance, your ability to work unorthodox hours, to handle complex deals under tight deadlines, to work well with different (sometimes difficult) personalities, to multitask and manage different projects, and to maintain a high level of customer satisfaction. Of course, this list could go on and on, depending on the expectations and areas of focus for your organization.

In a recent example, as a two-year credit manager who had achieved some notable results, I began to think what I wanted to "be" next, how I could exercise my creativity, and reach that next level of opportunity by adding the utmost value to my bank. I knew pretty quickly that I was a good two to three years away from assuming the next role because I had only been in my current role for two years. In addition, I knew that it would take time to create and put to work a transition plan for someone to take over my role.

My strategy was to first identify 2-3 opportunities that I would focus on choosing from. My interests were in the realm of creating opportunities that did not yet exist. On the one hand it is an exciting position to be in. On the other hand it is filled with uncertainties. After an inventory of my strongest and weakest suits, I came to realize that my core interests were in creating and growing new teams or turning around inadequately performing ones. I also decided that I wanted to focus either on business development or training. As part of my planning, I met with a number of people in my organization, including my mentors whose opinions I respect and trust. Through this soul searching process I fine-tuned and polished my vision as well as a possible plan of how to make my growth a reality.

This is still an ongoing endeavor as this book is being written, and I have not decided whether I want to focus on a business development effort or on training. Both opportunities will be of interest. What will ultimately determine my decision is which opportunity will allow for the most growth, learning, creativity, and impact within my company. In the end, I will focus on identifying the skills I need to acquire now to qualify for those positions. I will need to identify the people who can be of assistance in developing new skills as well as in helping me implement my strategy.

In conclusion, I want to offer a few final thoughts.

- Have a plan and of course have fun doing it! Our industry prides itself on having an inordinate number of cynics and fair bit of negativity. Enjoy what you do or strongly consider doing something else. As the President of Eastern Bank in Massachusetts noted at an event described earlier in this book, "If you don't love it, leave it."

- Be entrepreneurial and take opportunities as they come. Take advantage of them, be prepared and be willing to change your direction on the fly. The strategy can be to progress in the same direction but the means of achieving your goals can vary over time.

- Be persistent and stubborn yet flexible. Think of trees that bend in the wind, under the rain, and when covered by snow or ice during the winter months. When they are not flexible enough, they break. This is very much relevant in our personal experiences, including our professional lives.

- Listen for feedback but with a filter. If you are submerged in information without understanding it, you are not learning anything. There is not much intelligence in that approach. Always consider whether what you hear makes sense.

- There is an insightful Chinese proverb that says: "The person who says it cannot be done should not interrupt the person doing it."

Skill assessment, planning and execution

Inventory list of current skills/qualities			
Strengths			
Weaknesses			
Top 2-3 professional (or even personal) goals	1.	2.	3.
Top skills/qualities that will help achieve your professional goals	1.	2.	3.
Top skills/qualities to develop to achieve your professional goals	1.	2.	3.
Timeline			
Comments			

CHAPTER VII – LEARNING FROM THE BEST – THE ANALYST'S CREED

As you wrap up reading the section of moving beyond number crunching, I hope that you have begun to gain greater and greater appreciation for the less tangible, qualitative side of developing your credit skills (or Credit 102). I would like to conclude with the Analyst's Creed, which is nothing less than a list of best practices for aspiring to become a high-caliber credit professional.

- I will strive to get all numbers right on every deal and underwriting opportunity as they are the very foundation of high-quality credit analysis.

- I will not cut corners in putting numbers together, yet I will do it quickly and efficiently with a focus on what's relevant.

- I want to be known for the high quality of my work and for being eager to roll up my sleeves whether I am faced with a simple credit request or an exhausting and complicated transaction or task.

- I will work in a highly collaborative manner with lenders in helping get deals done, as we all get paid for closing deals. However, I will also stand my ground in getting a deal done with the highest level of quality and I will have the knowledge and confidence to persuade a lender that we need to do analysis in a certain way. I am a credit analyst first and foremost.

- I will always strive to find a proper balance between credit and business needs by being a credit analyst in my head and a business developer at heart.

- I will always aspire and make every effort to maintain a positive attitude as it is one of the few things I have control over in life. Life is too short to worry about why others behave the way they do. I only hope that my positive energy will help others have a better day.

- My every analysis will show what the key risks and mitigants are and why we should or should not do a particular deal. I will save my marketing skills to market to prospects and ensure that my credit reputation is never questioned.

- I will look at every challenge as an opportunity to make things better and to solve a problem.

- I will never stop learning and will remain humble no matter how far I advance in my career.

- Now ... write your own Creed!

Inspired, in part, by T. Berry Brazelton

PART II -

BUILDING A REPUTATION – YOU REAP WHAT YOU SOW

CHAPTER I – IT TAKES A LIFETIME TO BUILD AND A DAY TO LOSE

A reputation for a thousand years may depend upon the conduct of a single moment. Ernest Bramah

As you are working to build a successful banking career, moving beyond number crunching is only one of five pillars of your long-term success. Reputation is the second of the five pillars that will help you thrive and advance or will bring your opportunities for growth to a screeching halt. The key components of your reputation are as follows (there are many definitions out there – this is my take on it):

- Reputation for your industriousness (effort you put into your work)

- Reputation for the results you produce

- Reputation for your intelligence, ability to think outside the box and innovation

- Reputation for your attitude

- Reputation for honesty, fairness and ethics

- Internal reputation (how you are perceived within your organization)

- External reputation (how you are regarded in the market place)

The first five of the above are almost entirely what you accomplish and the last two are in part how you are perceived and are not 100% within your control.

What you should know first and foremost is that building your reputation is a lifelong endeavor. It will be build similar to building the foundation of a house, which is done one brick at a time. If you skip a section or cut a corner, structural issues over time can doom the entire structure. The good news is that you can help your reputation evolve by shaping it gradually and patiently. If things are not moving in the right direction, you often have the opportunity to correct your course. You must however have a lifelong commitment to reputation building.

Unfortunately, reputation can also be susceptible to hurricanes that can destroy it overnight. I am certain that looking back at history or even current economic events you can name presidents, CEOs, political figures, athletes, and business professionals who did doing something that hurt or financially injured others and ultimately ended up hurting themselves. Everything these individuals worked so hard to build was lost in a matter of days. Of course, you do not need to be a public figure or a well-known person to lose your reputation. All it can take is one grave mistake, and you are out of the game for good.

What you will realize fairly quickly is that commercial banking is a relatively small community. It could be subdivided into geographic, lines of business or other segments but those communities are tight-knit. As employee and employer loyalty continue to decline and as employee mobility continues to become more and more acceptable, the market-place of "employees at will" will grow further. More and more bankers are moving around from one organization to another with increasing frequency. The length of stay among younger generations is even shorter for two reasons: 1) younger individuals are part of the generational wave for whom 2-3 years with one employer is a long time; and 2) at lower levels in the corporate hierarchy there is less to hang on to, and it is all about learning as much as possible wherever possible. What was a taboo and a career-killing behavior a couple of decades ago, nowadays not even something employers and employees bat an eye over.

As a result, you see the same familiar faces as you move from organization to organization. It is always remarkable to attend networking events and see lots of former colleagues (besides the current ones!) and otherwise familiar faces. This is when it occurs to you that for all its size and breadth, the banking industry is quite small. As an example, the majority of bankers when making hiring (or sometimes other business) decisions call around to their network to inquire off the record about the individuals in question. What human resources personnel are unable to find out, or are scared away from talking about by lawyers, the network can discover pretty quickly. This is another example that strongly supports the argument for maintaining a reputation of the utmost quality.

The moment you begin working at an organization or even before, during the interview process, you have many eyes watching you. Every one of your colleagues one way or another is trying to figure out who you are, what you stand for and what you bring to the table. Part of it has to do with the fact that the quality of your work or the lack thereof is something that can affect them directly as well as the entire organization. I am not stating this to put extra pressure on you but you must be aware of this, especially since you are in the early years of your career as an analyst. You will interact with individuals who can have a tremendous impact on your prospects for growth and you will want to have the best chances for success.

I recall working with one analyst who had great strengths from a technical point of view. He could get the job done and meet the most demanding timelines. Unfortunately, his greatest weakness and therefore his opportunity to improve was his lack of motivation to adhere to some commonly expected behaviors, including timely arrival or presentable appearance. It was impossible to predict when this employee would show up for work. Some days it could be 10:00 a.m., while other days it could be 12:00 p.m. On numerous occasions he called in sick by midday of the day when he was actually sick. From the team and his manager's points of view, he was not reliable to say the least. Granted, he ended up getting the job done, but it was impossible to manage the team's workflow and take care of the credit needs that came up on the fly. In other words, he got the job done but on his terms, which is not the way to work in a team-centric setting. While the management team was pretty flexible in terms of attendance, this person's behavior was exceeding anything that could be called reasonable. Another challenge was the fact that this analyst did not adhere to the company-established dress code and personal grooming standards. For a reputable and high quality financial institution this was a great challenge, when we could interact face to face with clients and prospects at any moment.

As a result, this analyst almost never got a chance to meet with clients or was not the preferred choice. When it came to high visibility transactions, he was not the first choice either. Even as he made efforts to change from time to time, his colleagues held certain opinions and perceptions of him, which were very difficult to shake. In turn, the fact that his reputation appears to have stuck with him, his efforts to change were short lived. After a period of time he would revert back to his old habits, not realizing that changing a reputation is a long and painstaking endeavor. It is certainly not as long as a lifetime of developing and refining your reputation but certainly can take weeks, months and, in some instances, years. He simply did not understand what was required of him to change his reputation – a set of new behaviors, lots of patience and proving every single day that things had become truly different.

This brings us to the next and very important question in reputation building – what would you like to be known for? You need to realize that you cannot be known for everything. You may have a very wide range of positive qualities that serve you well every single day. However, there may be one or two qualities that you are especially proud of and that make you better than the majority of your peers. Rarely do you hear people referring to an individual as a person who excels in a long list of activities. This is perhaps why individuals like Michelangelo are born so rarely. It is more common that we are known for a few key qualities.

For example, after two or three years into my credit analyst career, I was first and foremost known for the ability to take the most complex deal under the tightest possible timelines and to get the job done and do it without complaining.

Here is a little exercise that gives you some key questions to provide a direction in reputation building. I would suggest taking your time when you go through these questions and periodically returning to revise your answers and directions as your career develops.

- What do you want to be known for and why? Make a list.

- How will these qualities and your reputation for these particular qualities help you in your learning and growth?

- Once you have created the list, it may be a good time to ask how far those skills are from where you would like them to be.

- The next question is to ask yourself how far your reputation is from where it needs to be, since having specific skills does not automatically mean that you are known for them. To answer this question you will need to reach out to others to assess how close or far your self-perception is from the opinions of others.

As an example, my answer to the question of what I want to be known for was quite similar to the Analyst Creed included at the end of the previous section. As a matter of fact, I continue to benefit from those skills and the reputation that they afford me, many years after I stopped working as a credit analyst. Make sure that you write your own version of the Creed that is linked with your own values, qualities and aspirations. Whenever possible, balance them with the general expectations in the industry.

As an example of the tremendous disconnect between someone's self-perception and their actual reputation as a credit analyst, I offer Jack, an analyst who once worked on my team. In my conversations with Jack even before becoming the team leader, I always felt that he had a solid knowledge of credit. His stance on many issues was firm, and he professed a strong degree of respect for credit quality. Beyond that, we never had a chance to work together. After I took the helm of the credit team and Jack began reporting directly to me, I very quickly realized that his advanced proficiency in credit was nothing more than a façade. First and foremost, he did not have a grasp of the UCA cash flow; what was relevant in analyzing a company's financial performance; how to ask lenders the right questions; how to write something more than what is known as elevator analysis; and many other skills. In sum, he lacked a knowledge of the fundamentals. Yet he was cocky and clueless about his shortcomings. The greatest challenge, however, for me and other members of the management team, was that he was dishonest. He would never admit that he was wrong and would try to argue a point that did not make sense. He would also misrepresent the qualitative components of what was behind a borrower's financial performance in his analyses. A common example of this misrepresentation was when Jack would state a reason behind a change in numbers or explanation of trends in his analysis, while he had not asked the lender and did not know what the real reason behind the change was. He was essentially guessing or, to put it plainly, making things up! Until you completely cornered him, he would not admit that he just did not know and therefore should not have made claims that were untrue.

After having maintained a façade of being knowledgeable about credit for a few years, Jack lost any credibility with the new management team and therefore with the bank. This is certainly the kind of situation that could have been fixed and Jack's reputation could have been repaired, if he himself had had the desire and commitment to do so. Sadly, Jack had no inclination and perhaps no ability to recognize his behavior for what it was. After a performance warning, Jack opted to leave the bank rather than work on improving his situation. He chose avoidance instead of dealing with a problem head-on.

As a final point, reputation risk is a key concern for every bank. Loss of reputation can lead to loss of customers, good standing in the community, and, in some extreme examples, law suits, financial losses and even bring about the demise of an organization. Banks are represented by their employees and reputation risk mitigation starts with them. For an organization with seemingly unlimited financial and non-financial resources, it is a lot easier than for an individual to deal with reputation risks and repairing damaged reputations. The rest of us do not have such a luxury. Use this as a learning experience – reputation is something we as individuals should be concerned about a lot more than businesses. As strong reputation is like good health - build it, improve it and benefit from it!

CHAPTER II – KNOW WHAT THE EXPECTATIONS ARE BEFORE YOU CHANGE THE WORLD

Fortune favors the prepared mind. Louis Pasteur

For better or for worse, our industry is not known to be the most progressive and is viewed by some as very slow to change. During my early years in banking I found it to be very conservative, hierarchical, lacking energy and dynamism, and quite often cynical. Fortunately, I am seeing more and more opportunities for the coming generations to do things differently. I am not sure whether it is because I am growing through the ranks and have more opportunities to have a seat at the table, rather than being stuck at lower levels without seeing the impact of my work. Perhaps it is because the industry is at a point where we will see generational turnover that will lead to significant changes (hopefully positive). Finally, perhaps an entrepreneurial approach to career development stands out in what is primarily a corporate industry with little focus on creativity, innovation and entrepreneurship. Whatever the reasons are, you will run into a roadblock of resistance to change and trying new approaches that make sense to you but not to others.

Regardless of how cutting edge or backwards any industry is, as you join it in the earlier stages of your career you are likely to see issues in a different light. If you feel out of place fairly quickly, maybe you are right. This is common when you join a new industry or a company and expect to have a voice that will be heard but realize that nobody cares about what you have to say. Many of us have seen time after time that individuals with little industry experience may be able to offer out of the box, creative solutions to existing problems. This commonly happens because those individuals have not had a chance to get used to how the business "should be" conducted and look at what's considered the "norm" in a different light. They are not yet jaded, so to speak. Seeing the reality differently is a unique skill and you should make sure that you preserve that skill. Unfortunately, joining an industry when you have not earned a voice is challenging. If you have limited work experience, you may also come across as a newbie and that could be the reason why your input is disregarded.

Hang in there! We have all been in those shoes. I was fortunate early in my career to meet a division executive (Norm DeLuca) who actually wanted to hear my thoughts and ideas and took the time to meet with me on several occasions. In retrospect, I can personally attest that some of my ideas were rather naïve and reflected a lack of essential work experience. This is one of the main reasons why inexperienced employees are rarely listened to. Nonetheless, Norm took the time to listen when others would not, and this was one of those gestures that gave my ideas reinforcement to weather the disregard until they had a proper environment in which to germinate. Such individuals are a rarity. It is more likely to have team leaders like the one I had the unfortunate privilege to work for in my first banking job, who would constantly ask how long I had been in the industry, as a "subtle" way to shoot down any ideas I had.

While you may quickly be able to notice flaws in how a banking business operates, try to balance this with finding positives. You probably have an endless level of energy to change things right away and find it incredible how the experienced people do not see the flaws in the system. To avoid getting frustrated and disenfranchised right away, focus on what's of utmost importance to you – to learn, develop and grow. Why worry and expend your energy on something you cannot change right away? First, focus on what is in your control. Second, write your ideas down, in what is commonly known as an idea wallet. It is possible that some of them will resurface later on, possibly even many years later. Third, identify that one idea that will have the greatest impact on your organization (remember, it is not all about you!) and build support for it to be considered and implemented. This last step may not be easy for more junior employees but it is achievable; the discussion of how it can be done is beyond the scope of this book however.

Below are a few thoughts that should help you deal with this challenge:

i) *What are the expectations of you? How are those expectations different from your expectations of yourself AND your expectations about your company?* This is one of those key challenges that you will need to overcome before you find your rightful place in your organization. Very often newer employees, especially the less experienced but full of energy individuals, ram into an impassable wall because they do not understand the rules of the game. In addition, this obstacle is even more impassable if you make everything about you instead of focusing on that fine balance of putting your organization first and then masterfully incorporating your own needs and aspirations.

ii) *Changes do not happen overnight – they take time, sometimes a lot of time.* I have heard quite often from junior to mid-career employees that the "old timers" are so hard to change. This fact alone makes upcoming generations' professional lives even more unbearable. Imagine my awe when as a new team leader who came in to define and implement a new course for a team of credit analysts, I ran into an incredible amount of resistance from a team of junior bankers in their twenties! This level of resistance and apathy toward a new direction could put any old timer's resistance to shame. This goes to show that resistance to change is a pretty generic response and is probably common regardless of tenure and age. As part of the slowness of change, you will also run into the "if it ain't broke, don't fix it" mentality. Sometimes it is appropriate but it often hides an unwillingness to improve continuously and look at ourselves critically.

iii) *The larger and/or the more bureaucratic your organization, the tougher it will be to implement any kind of meaningful change.* In a large organization, you will most likely be just a number. Yet, if you look on the positive side, large organizations are known for having significant resources to aid in learning and development as well as opportunities to move around and gain diverse experiences. With a bureaucratic organization, the challenge will be to learn as much as you can while building alliances to effect changes (if those changes are at all possible). The trick in such situations is to focus on the organization's goals and its key weaknesses in achieving those goals. This is where you can potentially hit the bull's eye.

iv) *You will need to prove your worth and earn your seat at the table.* As they say in the military, you will need to earn your stripes. This is an expectation because your colleagues who are already ahead of you had to do just that. This is your only chance to showcase the value you can add. Work hard, produce results, and you will be fine.

v) *Think of inconspicuous ways of changing reality.* You do not have to try to bring about changes in a radical way, especially if such a way is ineffective and does not get you where you need to be. A good example of various ways to bringing positive changes to life is the article titled "Radial Change, the Quiet Way" by Debra E. Meyerson, who presents four distinct approaches that can work for you and "…like steady drops of water … gradually erode granite."

A memorable example of working effectively and bringing about changes is a former lending colleague of mine who I will call Dan. Dan had a remarkable ability to work well with various individuals through all phases of loan prospecting, negotiations, underwriting, closing and account management. Dan understood that each person had a role to play in the system. He worked collaboratively with various areas of the bank to get what he needed to get a quality lending opportunity approved and booked. Everybody was happy to work with Dan because he did whatever was needed to get you what your process required, without an ounce of the attitude typical of many of his colleagues. As an example, before he sent loan documents for processing to the documentation team, he took the time to label them so that the team member could go through the documents quickly and efficiently. He was the only lender out of a few dozen lenders who took the time to make the processing team's job easier, and that team made everything possible and impossible to move his deal along in the queue.

One action-oriented quality Dan had was knowing when it was the proper time to resolve a problem. When he was actively engaged in working on a deal and time was of the essence, he did not try to use it as an opportunity to change the process or complain endlessly about an issue. He knew that it was best done after the deal is done and a client is taken care of. And, he always got things done with a positive attitude and smile on his face. On the polar opposite side, his many colleagues engaged in behaviors that brought them nothing but headaches – giving a hard time to individuals who were trying to help them, complaining every step of the way, seeing the lending job as a glass half-empty, and resisting anything and everything they disliked in the course of business. As a result, I have heard senior managers saying time and time again that if they could replicate Dan, the bank would have an incredible group of lending officers.

Ultimately, how you approach the idea of bringing about positive changes is up to you. You can do it in a way that will turn everybody against you or you can work within the system with its flaws and strengths. You can make it about the organization and then your career or about them versus you. Whichever path you choose, make sure you know what the expectations and rules of the game are. It is a 50% guarantee of your success.

CHAPTER III – PERCEPTION IS NOT EVERYTHING, BUT…

There is no smoke without fire. Idiom

There are a number of building blocks that create your image within your company, your market and even your own self-perception that are linked to your public image. This image is comprised of the quality of your work, your ability to deliver on goals and expectations, your attitude, and your reputation. It is the reputation or perception by others (also known as a personal brand) that I would like to focus on in this chapter. As Susan Hodgkinson concisely summed up in her book, *"The Leader's Edge"*, your brand strategy is an exchange of value that "is comprised of what you do, how you do it, the impact of your work on the bottom line, and who knows about it (besides you)." Nobody operates in a vacuum, and it is the interaction with your colleagues on a day-to-day basis that lays the foundation for your reputation. This reputation development can be actively managed. Unfortunately, in many instances we leave its development and evolution to chance rather than working to "control" it to send a message that we want the marketplace to hear.

You may say that as long as you do a great job, your reputation or your brand will fall into place and reflect all the great results you produce. The reality however is far from that. It is not uncommon for your reputation to be something completely different from what you want it to be. Remember that it is the interpretation by the market of various factual and non-factual pieces of information about you. A good example that comes to mind is an analyst who worked for my team in the past (let's call her Sara). Sara was an experienced analyst in terms of experience and years of work. She could take very complicated deals and produce a high-quality analysis. One of her key weaknesses was the fact that she was very argumentative.

As I continued to work with her and after numerous conversations trying to help her turn that weakness into a strength, I began to realize that argumentativeness may not have been her real intent. Instead, she may have been trying to question what she was being told, which is a sign of inquisitiveness and a desire to learn. However, she had no skill in channeling her reaction in way that she would listen to the opinions of others, know when to back off, and not get frustrated when conversations did not go in her favor (she just had to have the last word). As a result, Sara pretty quickly earned a reputation for being argumentative, combative and uncooperative. This was a very big issue in her performance because team work was the key to excelling and growing for any employee. Sara was labeled a non-team player by reputation, as someone who was not holding the bank's goals in focus. When an opportunity to apply for a position of senior credit analyst came about, her managers felt that her promotion would send the wrong signal to the rest of the team, one that said promotions are not tied to high performance. Additionally, there were significant reservations about her ability to produce high-quality work and be professional in the new role. If not for her shortcomings, Sara would have been the first eligible analyst on the team to apply for this opening. As a result, she was passed on this opportunity, which further exacerbated her attitude.

Now it is time to ask two important questions:

a) Do you know what your brand or reputation is within your organization and in the marketplace?

b) How is it different from the reputation you would like to have and why?

To assist you in this exercise, complete grids (i) and (ii) and make sure that you do it in that exact order (see the end of this chapter). Also consider reviewing grid (iii) after you complete (i) and (ii). Grid (i) will establish the top five qualities and values you want to be known for and hope to portray to the outside professional world. Grid (ii) will help you verbalize the qualities and value you feel your company and the market in general value and expect to see. Is there a disconnect between (i) and (ii)? This is where we continue to evaluate your perception of self and your perception of what the market values. Why do you think there is a disconnect, if there is one? How can you bridge the gap?

The next step is to answer question (a). This is where your own perception may not be enough. However, if your self-awareness and emotional intelligence are high enough, you should be able to summarize most of your market reputation correctly. First, consider reaching out to your mentors within and beyond your group who will be honest and objective in sharing this sensitive feedback. You may want to ask your peers for their opinions but those individuals have to be able to provide brutally honest feedback. A 360 review is yet another tool but not every organization may have the technology or culture to offer such evaluations. What you should be prepared for is potentially negative surprises and to use this information to your advantage, rather than getting defensive about it.

A personal experience to share goes back a few years ago when one of my employers provided a training session on personal branding. One assignment was a task similar to what I have outlined above. One bit of feedback that came to me personally was very unexpected and not flattering – a couple of individuals noted that I was too rigid, inflexible, and too set in my ways. It was especially disturbing to me because I thought of myself as being the complete opposite – flexible, open to feedback and able to change quickly, if necessary. Since then I have been able to change that perception and a big part of it was simply asking for examples of my behavior that would manifest those negatively perceived attributes. After a while I discovered that many of those examples were simply misunderstandings. All I needed to do was to build better relationships with my colleagues, expand the circle of my supporters, and provide a rationale for some of my actions. At that time I was somewhat resistant to the whole idea of branding because I associated it with being pretentious. In my frequent conversations with a former team leader, we kept talking about whether it was more important to focus on a "candy wrapper" rather than its content (i.e. choosing form versus substance). In the end, I came to the same simple realization many individuals have come to before me – if the market perceives me in a way that is contrary to what the intention is, I can choose to correct that perception (simple in many instances) or be stubborn and hope that someday I will be understood the way I want to be understood.

If you are trying to send a certain message and it is not being heard or your audience is getting a different impression, you may have significant challenges in developing, learning and advancing. The personal branding challenge is rather an extension of building your transferrable skills that I talked about earlier and then skillfully marketing those skills. You should not misinterpret the need to manage your personal brand as the need to be fake and disingenuous; far from it. It is a phenomenal skill to be aware of what's going on around you and to ensure that you are able to influence what others think of you. If you make the mistake of allowing others to shape the market perception of who you are, it is remarkable how well-intended actions and behaviors can be taken out of context and exaggerated as they get passed from one person to another. A word of caution: if you find yourself worrying more about how you are perceived than working on your development, it may be a good time to revisit your priorities.

I would like to conclude with an excerpt from Susan Hodgkinson's book, mentioned earlier (printed with permission from the author).

"Managing your brand involves the following:

- Knowing who you are and what's important to you, and connecting passionately to your work.

- Knowing which existing strengths to defend or grow, when to embrace feedback, and when to take steps toward self-improvement so you can be even better at what you do.

- Identifying and celebrating your uniqueness as the center of your brand value exchange. Do you own your own niche of excellence at work? If so, what is it and how do you continuously grow it? If not, why not and what are the implications of that for you and your business?"

Grid (i) - Top five qualities (including skills) and values you want to be known for

Qualities / values*	Rationale / reasoning
1)	
2)	
3)	
4)	
5)	

* In order of importance

Grid (ii) – Top five qualities / values (in your opinion) that your company / industry hold in high regard

Qualities / values*	Rationale / reasoning
1)	
2)	
3)	
4)	
5)	

* In order of importance

Grid (iii) - Top three to five qualities / values you are actually known for

Qualities / values*	Rationale / reasoning
1)	
2)	
3)	
4)	
5)	

* In order of importance

CHAPTER IV – THE VARIOUS "INTEREST GROUPS" – MULTI-TIER AUDIENCES TO PLEASE

When you fall down, it is your choice either to break down and cry or pick yourself up, dust yourself off and laugh the whole thing off.

It is interesting how some of our most sour life experiences turn out to be some of the best ones in retrospect. After the pain of challenges and struggles wears off, in some instances we look back at these experiences as a blessing in disguise and see a silver lining. As a more junior credit analyst, you will face numerous obstacles and frustrations. Some of them will be the following: focusing on the mundane and flat-out boring production component of the analyst's job; stresses of numerous deadlines; colleagues from lending and credit breathing down your neck; a feeling of being nobody, at the bottom of the barrel and in some instances getting little respect from your more senior peers, lenders and many others; demands from everybody and gratitude from nobody; not being able to see the big picture and feel the impact of your work; lack of client contact; and the need to please many different groups of individuals with different demands. It would be fair to conclude that some of these challenges are present in any job. Others, however, are more common to entry level jobs such as that of a credit analyst. These experiences will offer you an incredible learning opportunity, even if you do not appreciate them as you do the actual job. One of the reasons I am bringing up these issues in my book is because if you tune in and understand what is being discussed, you will take away from this experience much more than your peers will, and you will have a much better experience living through these challenges.

One of my very early professional experiences was my work as a brokerage representative at Fidelity Investments' Brokerage arm. If you have ever worked in a phone site environment, you know that it is a very demanding job with relatively little pay and high turnover. In the mid to late 1990s, you made approximately $25,000 annually and, if you wanted to make more, you would work a lot of overtime, which is exactly what I did. Imagine yourself being a rookie with a very demanding and knowledgeable customer base with many years of trading and market experience. They expect you to know everything, and you have to learn on the fly. They ride you hard, expect answers right away and have no patience whatsoever. Every time you place them on hold to find out answers, it aggravates them even more. Some customers are professional and respectful. Yet there are others who can be abusive, using profanities, and testing your patience like it has never been tested before. You, however, need to stay calm, respectful, get the correct answers, know your trade essentially on day one, and complete all your calls within a very few minutes (something you are measured for and the key to operating a profitable phone site). You spend your day on the phone; your days are filled with non-stop talking, thinking, finding answers, moving customers to the right areas, and, in the process, your team leader listens in on your calls to monitor their quality. That makes for a very exhausting day. When markets are down and the wait for phone representatives is longer, customers are losing or not making money, and everybody is highly irate and frustrated – you are the one taking those calls because you are at the front line of the company.

After over two years in such an environment, I left squeezed like a lemon and wanting to run away from my job, which I did. As the years passed however, I grew to appreciate those experiences more and more. I have learned to understand the market and its dynamics. I learned a tremendous number of customer interaction skills, including how to handle essentially belligerent people and stay calm and in control. I also learned to shake off the negativity that some of your customers can share with you. Finally, I came to understand and appreciate that job for its production-oriented environment, where employees need to handle close to a hundred calls a day in some instances and take care of their customers' needs with the same high quality and consistency all day long. This experience gave me a solid foundation to deal with the production nature of credit and lending jobs, working on the sales side spending lots of time on the phone and talking in person to C-level executives of prospective borrowers, and to manage time well, working on time-sensitive and numerous issues that needed to be addressed right away. I am sure that many of you have already had similar tough jobs, and you will likely grow to appreciate many of those experiences as time passes.

Similarly to my experiences at Fidelity Investments, the credit analyst job has many tough challenges to deal with that can and will be a remarkable "school" for you. If you "live" through this learning experience and produce the highest quality results with utmost attitude, it will undoubtedly allow you to be successful in many other roles (from credit to lending and far beyond). One valuable experience is working for and pleasing various audiences and various customer levels. Below is the chart that sums up many but by no means all client groups you have to take care of as a credit analyst.

The groups that you will interact with and "service" the most will likely be lenders, your team leader, (indirectly) customers of the bank, and credit and lending managers. Overall, these are quite a few "customer" groups to please, each with their own demanding expectations. You may ask, – who matters the most? There is really no straight answer to this puzzle. What you have to remember is that you represent credit as a credit analyst and you will need to reflect the balance of your organization's credit and lending (sales) culture while writing well-balanced *credit* analyses. It is not uncommon for analysts in their zealousness to impress lenders to cross that line to forget that they represent credit first and foremost and that they are independent and objective thinkers. When undesired crossover experiences take place, I always remember from my lending days what my team leader, Rob Nentwig, used to periodically remind me: "Always remember that you represent the bank and it pays your paycheck." I would add to that: "Always remember that your paycheck comes from the credit department of your organization." Never ever forget that your purpose is to act in the best interest of your employer (within ethical and legal boundaries, of course).

The fact that I listed your team leader second does not mean that lenders would supersede your direct supervisor. Your team leader along with the rest of the credit management team will set goals, the strategy to achieve those goals and the direction that the team and you personally will follow. Additionally, she or he will review your write-ups, coach and advise you on improvements needed, provide formal and informal training, be what I would call your Chief Cheerleading Officer, and act in many other roles depending on your operation's setup. A good team leader will listen to your feedback and suggestions (as long as they are made professionally and respectfully) but ultimately that individual will set the direction for the entire team.

A few times in my career both as a credit manager and as an analyst I have experienced situations when an analyst loses touch with reality and begins to argue about the direction or directly challenge his or her supervisor. Leaving aside the actual issues in question, in most cases this is not a battle you can win. As an up and coming professional you ought to develop a keen sense for when to ask questions, how to understand a situation in its entirety and how to channel your feedback and concerns. Beyond that, you will also need to know when to fall in with your team and your team leader and understand that you are a part of the bigger picture and greater vision. Don't forget that managers in lending and beyond are also looking at these kinds of behaviors. No one wants to have an employee who is not capable of following directions or who gets the job done with numerous arguments and makes the manager prove every single time that the job needs to be done and needs to be done certain way. This is when some analysts may wonder why a lending team leader passed on his or her candidacy to join the team while that analyst went "above and beyond" in providing credit analysis the way lenders expected. This happens because lending managers do not look for portfolio managers and lenders who can write marketing documents but rather individuals who know credit well and have the integrity and confidence to enforce credit standards. Business development can be taught to experienced credit employees. It is a lot harder to go the opposite way for experienced sales professionals.

CHAPTER V – YOU CAN'T BE KNOWN FOR EVERYTHING

Many of us have diverse skills, interests and experiences. Only some of them tend to be utilized in our daily work, while others get left behind dormant and underutilized. Which ones should you focus on developing and which ones should you be known for? (These are not automatically the same.) The direction will depend on what and how you are doing now, what your organization needs, what the market and economic realities are and the career direction you want to pursue in the near future. Part of your agenda will also be ensuring that what you are good at is also what you are known for.

Our industry is highly efficient at labeling or typecasting individuals from the very first days of their careers. The most unfortunate one I have come across is labeling us as credit (analytical, numbers-cruncher) and lending (sales, networker, business developer) professionals. I could never stand such typecasting in part because I was always trapped by it and it always limited my career progression. Although some may argue that the majority of people can be placed either into credit or lending tracks, there are a number of individuals who are rooted in credit and yet tremendously enjoy and are successful in business development. Their careers consist of movements back and forth between credit and lending functions and they often gravitate toward marrying both. Alas, the industry does not always comprehend that the two can go hand in hand. Many organizations are just incapable of taking advantage of such talent. I would refer to such personalities as "credit minds with a passion for sales."

I recall being a senior level (generalist) analyst, interviewing for an analyst position in an ABL unit of a superregional bank. During the interview it was pointed out a number of times that I did not have ABL experience at an ABL team, to which I responded that I had strong credit skills and experiences and that learning the finer details of ABL lending would not be a challenge. Additionally, I have underwritten a number of ABL-type deals at non-ABL specialty teams. Unfortunately, the fact that I was not a pure ABL analyst was one of the key reasons why I did not get that job. The hiring manager did not have the ability to see beyond the predetermined profile he was looking for. Fast-forward to less than 3 years later, when I was reviewing the portfolio of that same team leader, in a credit review capacity after I made a career switch to that same bank. That ABL team leader was extremely surprised to see me again, in my then current role, including the fact that I very correctly pointed out a number of underwriting errors and issues made by analysts, portfolio managers, and relationship managers under his guidance. Who knows if those mistakes would have been made if I were given a chance to take that analyst opportunity?

So, how do you steer clear of the typecasting landmines, differentiate yourself for your key qualities, and keep the message about your qualities clear and highly focused? Below are four simple steps that I recommend.

1) Choose the top two to three skills you want to be known for and focus on developing them.

If you do not have clarity about who you are and what you are good at, then there is no way you will be able to communicate this to yourself, your employer and the market. Naturally, if your issue is a lack of key strengths or qualities that will be valued by your institution and its competitors, then you have a challenge ahead of you to build those skills first. There is nothing worse than a) having a reputation for certain strengths and not being able to prove them in action or b) not having any strengths to be known for and therefore being regarded as unremarkable and average. This is a guaranteed way to torpedo your career and reputation.

As you move through the process of verbalizing your key strengths, compare them to your interests and career goals to ensure that they offer maximum growth and results. If not, you may end up acquiring, developing and honing skills that are not very relevant to what you want to achieve.

2) Make sure that your brand and reputation in the industry are known and well-regarded for those two to three skills.

To continue the discussion from prior chapters, this task is a) knowing what your brand or reputation is in the market and b) having a marketing plan to spread the word or repair the reputation that is aligned to your true strengths and goals. I call it a balance between constant maintenance, evolution, diagnosis, intervention, and prevention. Spreading the word about your strengths is done, among other ways, through a combination of the results of your daily work, the results of your work as they are communicated (rumored) by others, your communication of those strengths while networking and interviewing, and the track-record of your growth as communicated by your resume.

3) Change the skills and messages the marketplace receives from time to time to reflect your career evolution.

Nothing is set in stone in your career. As some research shows, it has become more and more common for people to have two, three or more careers in their lifetime. It has also become more acceptable to both change careers and move between different organizations with increasing frequency even in a conservative industry as (commercial) banking. If you feel that you could choose two to three career tracks within banking at any given time, it is perfectly fine to be open to more than one career direction, depending on which one offers a greater possibility of growth (unless there are clear signs and evidence of a lack of focus on your part and not knowing what you want to do). I find myself in such a position all the time; so do many other people. Being at crossroads is natural. Again, as long as you know why you are interested in those tracks and how you would go about moving toward those goals, it probably means that you have more than one talent and interest. There is nothing wrong with being opportunistic when it comes to managing your growth as long as you produce strong results in your current job and demonstrate a flexible and extremely positive attitude.

To repeat, do make sure that your career planning and the execution of your plan deals with an analysis of relevant skills and experiences, including the skills you have, the quality of those skills, improvements needed and any new skills you need to acquire. Whenever your career direction changes, part of your marketing plan should be to communicate to relevant people the change in focus, direction, and qualities that go along with the change.

4) Eradicate any attempts to be labeled, especially if it is not in the direction you desire or if you doubt that it is something you want to be known for during the rest of your career.

This step will require a combination of persistence, patience, diplomacy and strong communication skills. For organizations and individual managers it is so much easier to box you in because it is the path of least resistance. They do not need to worry about what is important to you or to allocate resources for your development but rather choose what is of value to them – having a long-term employee who stays put because he or she has nowhere else to go.

A very recent example from my own experience is gaining the label of a "teacher" or a "professor." A number of my colleagues have observed that I seem to have a talent for training credit analysts, among other professionals. Training is something I have always enjoyed doing although I was not interested in becoming a professional trainer. Instead, I drew particular satisfaction from using my creativity to design training solutions to solve business problems and help other professionals maximize their career opportunities. To me every good manager, lender, mentor, and leader should have good training and coaching skills. Additionally, my concern with being labeled as a teacher was as follows: Unfortunately, in business circles the teacher reputation is commonly and negatively associated with an individual who cannot do it him- or herself and therefore teaches others how to do it (i.e. a theoretician). If I were to let this reputation prevail, it might have precluded me from holding business development and other roles. I was able to manage the potential negatives quite well, which was possible in part because I recognized that this particular reputation was not to my benefit.

Now to bring this back to the field of commercial credit analysis, figure out what talents will make you stand out and help you have a rewarding career. You may want to use a combination of skills and talents that you already have as well as develop the ones that are highly valued by your organization and the industry in general. We live in an age of limited attention spans. As a consequence, it is highly important to keep your current and former colleagues, your potential employers and the overall market aware of what you want to be known for. This principle will serve you well, not only in the role of a credit analyst but also any other role you will pursue. For example, when I was a commercial lender, my goal for every meeting with a prospect or a network member was to leave him or her with a memory of two to three key facts that would allow that person to a) remember me easily and b) allow me to stand out from all their other lender contacts. What are you known for? Do you know? What do you want to be known for? Don't forget that you can't be known for everything!

Developing a focused skill set

a) Current key skills / qualities	b) Skills you are known for	c) If a) and b) do not match, action required	d) Skills highly valued by your company	e) Skills highly valued by your industry	f) If a) does not match d) and e), action may be	g) Skills you need/want to develop

Strategies to deal with c, f, and g

Goal	Strategy	Timeline	Comments

CHAPTER VI – LEARNING FROM THE BEST – LESSONS FROM A BANKING EXECUTIVE

On November 05, 2008, the RMA Young Professional Group held its 4th Annual "Executive Series" event, which brings together top executives from Massachusetts-based financial institutions with members and supporters of the RMA Young Professionals Group. Our typical target audience is junior to mid-career financial services professionals. We do not define ourselves in terms of a particular age group and everyone is welcome. Our events are also attended by more senior bankers and finance professionals who enjoy the opportunity to interact and share their experiences and knowledge with upcoming generations and future leaders.

Our feature speaker at that meeting was Robert Rivers, President of Eastern Bank. Mr. Rivers has a banking career going back to 1982. He opened the event by saying that his hope was to share not only a biographic account of his career highlights, but he was eager to share the lessons he learned over the years and was hopeful that the attendees would take advantage of them.

Mr. Rivers recounted that he grew up a shy boy. His mother noticed this early and made an effort to push him in front of people to help him become comfortable being in the public eye. After high school, he really wanted to attend an art school for his undergraduate studies, but could not afford the tuition. One of his early jobs was bagging groceries in the early 1980s, which he admittedly had a lot of fun doing. Instead of going to art school, Mr. Rivers got a job at Randolph Savings Bank in 1982. To his father, who wanted him to get business experience, a teller job at a bank seemed like a good opportunity. Mr. Rivers didn't think so and even unsuccessfully tried to botch the interview arranged by his dad. Not only did he work as a teller during the day, but he also cleaned that branch and a branch of a different bank across the street in the evening. The work environment was clean overall and presented opportunities for learning social lessons that he draws upon even today. One of them is treating everyone with courtesy and respect.

Mr. Rivers pointed out that throughout his career he had good mentors who helped him guide his career. One of them, Bill Burke of Stonehill College, taught him to always aim very high so that, if he fell short, he would still go farther than he otherwise would have. In retrospect, Mr. Rivers said that he missed his goal of being the president of a bank by only two years.

Bob Rivers' career highlights entailed the diversity of roles he held at different banks. After Randolph Savings he joined Old Stone Bank, which provided the opportunity to work in a small group of six in corporate planning that offered exposure to several functions of finance and strategic planning. Among several lessons that he learned, three in particular stood out:

1) Read and learn all that you can as knowledge breeds enthusiasm and creates opportunities;

2) Avoid cynicism, as it is a cancer that will only limit you; and

3) Be conservative on credit – it's about the only thing that can kill a bank.

While Mr. Rivers enjoyed a variety of assignments, he always thought about the next steps he might take. At Old Stone, he was already thinking about graduate school. After grad school, he spent 14 years with M&T Bank in a variety of roles, from product management and marketing to commercial lending and retail banking. During that time he learned that a diversity of experiences makes you a stronger senior manager and a better teammate. It also expands your opportunities. Mr. Rivers went on to say that you can always learn something from your boss, whether good or bad one.

The overall presentation was filled with honest and sincere anecdotes that Bob Rivers drew from his career experiences and was generous enough to share. This is not something less senior professionals have the opportunity to experience daily. One observation was particularly timely given the present economic environment – there a point after which the bank runs management rather than the other way around. Ultimately, we should remember that we make our own luck. His attitude toward work is simple – if you don't love it, leave it!

Mr. Rivers wrapped up the event with three pieces of advice:

- Find something you have a real passion for and go for it.

- Don't stop at one thing.

- Do good things and good things will happen. Just work hard, learn and read as much as you can, and don't focus on the money.

PART III –
FIND YOUR PLACE ON THE PLANE

CHAPTER I – BETWEEN MEDIOCRITY AND EXCELLENCE – THERE IS A PLACE FOR EVERYBODY

Sometimes there is too much focus on career progression and the pressure to be the best. Maybe this is a side effect of Western consumerism or something else altogether. Whether it is a real problem or not is not the subject of this book but at one point or another in our personal and professional lives we have all been exposed to this "peer pressure" to climb up the corporate ladder (at times self-imposed). Do we have to be the best in everything we do, achieve everything there is to achieve and have all there is to have, in terms of both possessions and business titles? The answer is absolutely "no." There is no law that you have to act in such manner. There is no such expectation from every organization or a social expectation for all citizens. It is further acceptable and satisfactory to not want to be the best of the best on your job, because you may have other aspirations in life and would want to apply yourself in other spheres that have nothing to do with your professional career. Even if you have no aspirations for whatever your personal and professional reality is, that is fine too. It is all a matter of choice as well as living with the consequences of your choices, however positive, negative or neutral.

Corporate ladder-climbing aside, what I and many other people believe in is the constant desire and effort to self-improve, become better, and further our evolution as bankers, business people and individuals. It is unfortunate that a common description of people who are trying to live balanced, sustainable, environmentally prudent and ethical lives is that they are spiritual weirdoes, eccentrics or tree-huggers. It is particularly out of place because a well-balanced and sustainable approach to doing business and living used to be regarded as taking care of "the hand that feeds you." This was the motto of hundreds of generations, and it served them well. Thus, if you are a driven individual and want to constantly learn, improve and grow AND want to do it without being a shark, it is absolutely possible. Some individuals I have talked to stated that they want to advance professionally but do not want to do it at any cost. Fortunately, you do not have to do this to achieve good results.

For instance, when I became the manager of a credit team at one particular bank, my goal and that of the rest of the management team was to build an A-level, high performing team that attracted and developed only high-achievers. I realize that this profile is not for everybody. Naturally, not everybody was attracted to our group, and we were very quickly able to weed out candidates who were not the right fit for the bank. As long as we as managers were honest and set very clear expectations during the recruiting and hiring process as well as in our day-to-day team management, we were able to build the team we wanted and offer career paths for our credit analysts. Although the team we built became a high-performing team with significant improvements from where it had been for many years, analysts rarely worked long hours or stayed nights and weekends (although I am certain that some managers or lenders would have loved to see that happen as a sign of commitment and drive). It does not mean that the job was not stressful and did not require the utmost commitment and performance. As a matter of fact, it did. Nonetheless, it still allowed for a fairly balanced approach to work and personal life.

Now it is your turn to choose where you would like to be on the straight or not-so straight line below. I call the set of two lines below the "career performance plane" which consists of input and output.

|---|
No focus on the job | All about the job
No commitment | Utmost commitment
No drive | Highly driven
Little to no development and improvement | Constant improvement

Then draw a 90-degree line from the line above to the one below. Your career progression will likely reflect the efforts you put into your work and development and the results you produce.

|---|
No advancement opportunities | Being consistently promoted
Little compensation improvement | High, above-average comp
Stuck in dead-end job | Lots of changes, excitement

There are lots of jobs out there and lots of opportunities. As very insightfully noted by Barry Schwartz in his book, *the Paradox of Choice*, having choices can be liberating and inspiring but having more choices than one can handle and settle on can be very disorienting. If you do not have the skills and patience to identify career paths that are aligned with your interests and steer toward them, then you risk making erratic and irrational career choices that can lead to aimless jumping around. This is not the way to achieve a balanced and satisfactory professional life. This is why one of your early challenges will be to decide how much effort you want to put into your work, what you want to achieve, how hard you want to work for it and how smart you are about it, as well as how high your goals and aspirations are.

As noted earlier, do not be frustrated if you want to reach a certain professional level in banking (or beyond) but are far behind your goals because you not able or willing to put in the effort and generate results. It is not the industry's, your company, or your manager's fault that there is a disconnect between your desires and your contribution to making your dreams a reality. Your employers may not be good at providing direction and helping you uncover your path to success but neither do they have to be. Outstanding managers and leaders can help guide your advancement but they are the minority. It is your responsibility to pave a path to professional and personal growth!

A very good example would be a mid-career analyst I had the opportunity to work with a few years ago. He had a decent credit training background and a number of noteworthy experiences to put on his resume. His expertise and high potential to someday become a good lender were noted by many managers at the bank. Despite a wide variety of strengths, one major flaw was all it took to stall his "career train." Firstly, he always thought that he knew it all or certainly made it look like he knew more than he actually did. Secondly, he thought that he had more experience than his more senior colleagues and that he belonged to that higher professional level, even more than they did. Therefore, he expected unquestionable recognition of his expertise but was himself unable to recognize the expertise and experience of others. Thirdly, he was not willing to put an extra effort into his job. The extra effort had to do with extra hours and, at a minimum, meeting or exceeding performance expectations for every analyst on the team.

This analyst was extremely unhappy because he felt that his career went dormant on him. In conversations with others he talked about all the great qualities and experiences he had, which should have allowed him to advance years before. Yet, he was stuck as an analyst without any prospect for growth. My conclusion was that he wanted to be somebody but for some reason did not want to work for it; in my assessment, at least a part of the problem was that he was lazy. His career stalled, and it was nobody's fault but his own.

I was speaking with one of my mentors about this challenge, and he had something similar to recount about his team. His analyst ended up leaving the bank without comprehending that he was the reason why his career did not progress as desired. That individual used to roll in by close to 9 am and then walk out with a few of his friends to get coffee. By the time they would be back, it would be 9:30 am or later. The day was over by 4:45 or 5 pm. This would not have been an issue for my mentor, if this analyst was able to do all his work within the hours he worked. The reality was far from that. After this analyst left the bank, another bank's recruiter called my mentor to obtain a reference on this individual (the analyst actually gave the prospective bank my mentor's name, hoping for a good reference after his subpar performance!). Not wanting to say something particularly bad about the analyst, he noted that "he was a heck of an analyst." I am not sure if the recruiter understood the meaning of this reference, but I hope that you will never find yourself in the position of being categorized as a "heck of an analyst," especially if that's not your goal.

In summary, as you are deciding where to fit on the "career performance plane," remember that results matter just as much as the efforts. Efforts are definitely good to see. However, if after a while they are still not producing the desired results, you need to come up with a new strategy because something is not working. You also need to decide for yourself how far above and beyond you are willing to go to achieve your goals. Finally, look at your team and your organization to better understand expectations for you and everybody else. Is it the right place for you? For instance, if you are a part of a high performing team but for you your job is just a job and the means to achieve something that takes place after you leave your place of work, you may want to consider switching jobs. Your team can make you look mediocre, even if you post average performance acceptable on many other credit teams.

We all talk too much about results, however. In the race to produce and achieve, we work hard to reach our goals. It is equally important to enjoy the journey itself or your life will seem like a race track, sometimes a very miserable one. Speaking from experience, some of us tend to be perfectionists and very results-driven individuals. Give us something challenging to do, and we will work as hard as possible to achieve it, especially if we find the goal personally appealing. The downside of this zeal is that it is never enough. The journey toward the final goal becomes less relevant. The achieved goal is not so important either, the moment it is achieved. We never pause to celebrate because we already have our eyes set on something else – the next target. Do not get caught in this vicious cycle. Take your time to enjoy the road of growth. Recoup your lost energy and reenergize! Pause and celebrate each accomplishment!

CHAPTER II – JOB VERSUS CAREER PATH

Is there a difference between a job and career path? Which should you pick and why should you care? There are a couple of interesting questions that you will run into during your career as a credit analyst. I compare a job with a transactional relationship at a bank. Your bank may want to lend but it does not get deposit and cash management, residential lending, investments management, and other relationships. It is just a quick deal – a transaction. If you are a relationship bank, it only makes sense to do the deal if it is priced high enough. A career path is most commonly something that has a long-term direction. It is a relationship. It will include many different jobs but there is an overall direction, a natural progression and therefore the opportunities that come with them. This is the difference between the two. To define "career path" as a term, I would pick "a flexible line of progression through which an employee moves during his or her employment with an organization" (a definition I found on www.johnwiley.com).

On the second question of which you should prefer and why, I would answer that it depends. The term "job" may have a negative connotation. Why would you want a transaction, right? Well, let's suppose that you find a financing opportunity that offers a very nice return for a reasonable amount of risk. You might not want a transaction as a regular occurrence but might consider one, if the terms are very attractive. I look at the choice between a career path and a job in a similar manner. A particular job may offer a very attractive opportunity to learn and develop. It might not have a long-term future but may offer something other jobs and career tracks do not. Another rationale for taking a job could be a next-step growth opportunity that the current career path does not offer or does not offer fast enough. Thus, you make a strategic decision to take a job. For example, a peer of mine had an opportunity to do a rotation in work-out for just one year. This was a fantastic development opportunity for her that soon led to the next, higher level assignment. Yet another reason is money. This is not the most extensive list but jobs do have their place when a career track is not available or does not offer sufficient return on your time invested. Jobs are more relevant in this economic environment when so many bankers are unemployed. Most of us have held jobs that were just jobs, taken job offers that were just job offers, and will continue to do so. Our circumstances will determine our behavior.

Career tracks are however what many people seek and so should you. They offer continuity and stability and hopefully challenges, growth opportunities, learning, and income potential. In the early stage of your career, you are more likely to run into jobs that are just jobs because your goal is to learn as much as possible, develop, and grow. While the amount of money you make is very important since you make less early in your career and every penny matters, your first priority is to find a company that provides a good learning platform. Analysts tend to be content with a lower salary, within reason, in exchange for growth prospects in the future.

In this regard, you may also find my article titled "The New Generation of Bankers. Are we Ready?" of interest, which is provided immediately after this chapter. It supports the conjecture that the focal point for career decisions for junior professionals is more about training, learning, and development. Jobs can do just fine in satisfying those needs. Another reason for choosing jobs that are just jobs is that earlier on in your professional days you may not know what you want to do in the long run. It can take time to work in several roles in several organizations before you know what you really want to do. Does this mean that you should not look for career paths from the very beginning? Absolutely not! If you find them and if they meet your goals, take advantage of those opportunities!

On average, you are more likely to move around earlier in your career. The rate at which employees change jobs has been accelerating over the years, even in banking. Now it is more and more common to see analysts work a year or two in one organization and then the next one. Even ten to fifteen years ago, if you were to have several organizations under your belt in less than 10 years, most banks would have passed on you as a candidate in favor of others. This is not the case anymore however, which is how people like me have jobs and then career tracks. Nonetheless, too much jumping around with poor rationale for switching is frowned upon and can cost you a prospective opportunity. Your frequent job changes can be interpreted as a lack of career direction or as underperformance that caused your previous employers to not want to promote you from within.

In general, large organizations are better than the small ones for your early training as an analyst. Those organizations tend to have substantial resources and credit training programs (although those are disappearing too). There is nothing better to the ear of many credit managers than the phrase "formal credit training." Additionally, if a large institution wants to develop its employees and retain them, it can offer opportunities to move around, which can be crucial to cross-training and finding out what you really want to do and what you are really good at (these are not always the same). Again, this does not happen all the time. The typical downside to a large company environment is that you are likely to be just a number, and it is hard to get noticed in a crowd.

Smaller institutions are anecdotally better at appreciating individuals and providing a fertile ground for development for experienced credit analysts. Such companies may be able to offer competitive compensation for the talent they cannot develop in-house. This is why so many bankers go through a large bank training system and eventually settle down at smaller institutions. They are somebody there and can add value based on their expertise. One common downside to smaller banks is the lack of growth and further development opportunities, especially if they do not have aspirations to grow and evolve. Somehow organizations forget that employees need to develop over the course of their entire careers, not just in the beginning. This is when smaller bank jobs and career tracks can turn into cushy and stable employment opportunities that lack learning, challenge and excitement. Again, these are average scenarios, and there are exceptions.

Remember that a substantial part of your growth can and will depend on your team and your team leader, but the organization, its culture and growth pace do play a role. You may work for a remarkable bank that gets accolades for its financial strength and employee focus but, if you get stuck with a rotten team and an incapable supervisor, your life will be miserable and your career will not go far. Yet, I have worked at dysfunctional and underperforming organizations that had entrepreneurial teams and managers who helped me further my career like no other teams would. Therefore, I recommend looking first and foremost at the team and your prospective team leader.

Not every organization is able to offer formal or even less formal career paths. It does not make it a bad organization but puts it at a disadvantage in attracting quality employees for the long term. If you have a career path, it does not have to mean staying at the same organization forever but if that organization is able to keep you challenged, there is nothing wrong with working for such a company for a long time. If your organization does not seem to provide the potential to move upward, take advantage of my personal mistakes and do not run away from a non-advancing career right away. Instead, you should attempt to explore growth opportunities with your management. If you don't take action and just switch jobs, the problem of your not taking initiative and taking charge of your career may not go away simply by changing companies. If your efforts to design a career path in your current company do not produce results, then move to plan B and begin to look around. In the meantime, do not forget to have a positive attitude and continue to produce results. You will be much less miserable in the job you do not love and will leave a good impression in case you need references from your current employer or if you work with the same individuals again.

For somebody who has moved around quite a bit, worked at jobs that were just jobs, and who finally found several good career tracks, I will admit that it is not uncommon to think that the grass is always greener on the other side. That is not a reason to switch! Think in terms of the context of your career and what's good for you in the long run. This skill will come handy as you become more experienced. I recall a friend of mine who worked very hard his entire career to develop a career track and direction for himself. He would structure it in 2-3 year rounds or assignments. He would do a terrific job in each of his roles first and foremost. He knew exactly what his final goal was. He also knew what experiences he needed to gain. His first move would be to line up the opportunities he wanted within the organization he was working for. However, if that organization did not offer that next move opportunity, he would very strategically make a move to the next, always higher role every two to three years. By his early 40s, he was already the COO of a biotech firm.

As a final thought, until you are in the later stages of your career, design your career track around the following needs:

- Need to learn and develop

- Need to grow

- Need for challenge

- Need for better flexibility in life / balance

- And only then, need for money

CHAPTER III – THE NEW GENERATION OF BANKERS. ARE WE READY?

Copyright of the RMA and the author

Community Banking: Viewpoint

THE NEW GENERATION *of* Bankers Are We Ready?

Drawing on his 10 years in the financial services industry, the author seeks to give voice to the views and thoughts of today's young bankers. He hopes to facilitate a dialog between young bankers and their more senior counterparts that can lead to rewarding, lifelong career opportunities. Before writing this article, which is directed at management, Berdiev conducted a survey of young bankers across the country. Readers are encouraged to respond with their reactions.

by **Dima Berdiev**

After nearly four years as a commercial lender, Charles W. felt his career had reached a crossroads. *Should he leave the bank? Leave banking altogether?* Many thoughts ran through his mind:

- With industry-wide cuts in training, I'm beginning to doubt I'll have an opportunity to learn more in coming years.
- On-the-job training is limited at best. Work keeps getting piled on me, and there isn't time to learn something new.
- I don't have a mentor, and people are just too busy to offer any guidance.
- My bank's idea of challenging employees seems to be in the amount—not diversity and complexity—of work.
- I don't see any clear-cut, long-term career path.
- I just want some clarity, direction, and opportunities, but there's no way to communicate that. Everybody likes me because I don't complain and I have a positive attitude. When other employees said they were dissatisfied with where they were, their advancement opportunities evaporated.

89

Restless Banker Syndrome

While Charles W. is fictitious, I know many like him in the banking industry, especially among the newest generation of bankers. These individuals feel like their careers are on autopilot, flying in uncertain directions. Further, their expectations and career goals may seem irreconcilably different from those of their esteemed, tenured colleagues, who often are the ones in authority. Intergenerational misunderstandings, tensions, lack of mutual respect, and even conflicts are not uncommon.

Admittedly, there are regional differences in "restless banker syndrome." For example, cities or rapidly developing suburban areas tend to offer more opportunities to move between firms, while rural regions may mean fewer options and lead to longer average tenure with one organization. In addition, large banks may offer more opportunities to move within its different groups, which can serve as its own retention tool.

The question remains: We can guess at the reasons for restless banker syndrome, but what's the real story?

A Survey to Support the Conjecture

Assuming that banks aren't happy about a revolving-door approach to employment, I surveyed about 50 junior to mid-level bankers across the country to validate my suspicions. I wanted to find out what drives and motivates future generations of bankers in their career decisions. And yes, the key message I heard is that they are pretty disappointed in the lack of career development and feel that their thoughts and feedback to their managers commonly fall on deaf ears.

Before you read more about my survey, why not think about conducting your own? Ask yourself these questions:

- How many times have I lost a rising-star employee because I was so consumed with meeting departmental goals that I didn't find time to share my knowledge, advice, or feedback?
- Has that person asked for my support to explore career options (not to switch, but to create a long-term plan) by learning more about groups within the bank? Has my organization made it all but impossible for that person to learn and understand what

else is out there and, as a result, lost a good employee?

- How many times have I opted to hire a person with the right number of years in a particular job rather than train an existing employee? (Did you know that, in the process, you might have undermined your tenured employees by offering the newcomer more money and a more senior title?)

The fixes to these problems are relatively simple. However, you might have lacked time, resources, the desire—or any combination of the three—to listen and implement the necessary changes. You're not alone. As an industry, our track record isn't so good.

Survey findings. This survey of junior and mid-level bankers focused on two areas:
1. Why participants decided to search for a new job: a) compensation; b) expectations/promise of better growth and/or learning opportunities; c) an organization or team they liked and wanted to work for; or d) other factors (with a request to provide details).
2. Feedback the participants would like to share with their

We can guess at the reasons for "restless banker syndrome," but what's the real story?

Chapter III – The new generation of bankers. Are we ready?

The New Generation of Bankers: Are We Ready?

organizations' senior management and the industry's executives: what management can and should do to keep the respondents dedicated, interested in their work, and willing to stay in one organization for a longer period of time.

As expected—and contradicting the common belief—compensation is not the primary reason people switch jobs. Young professionals want to see their career options and to move in their chosen direction as a reward for their dedication and hard work. They want their annual reviews and annual performance plan to incorporate this aspect. In addition, a considerable number expressed interest in cross-training and the opportunity to do a rotation in another department, even if only to shadow a colleague for a few days.

Younger bankers want management to provide fair and objective feedback, clear goals, honesty, and open communication. They also expect management to honor any promises made. Last but not least, they want mentorship opportunities with their senior colleagues and a chance to grow within their organizations through a combination of on-the-job and classroom training.

Where Banks Miss the Mark

Banks—whether community, regional, or large—do not commonly take advantage of opportunities available to retain young professionals more effectively. Instead, they find additional ways to shoot themselves in the foot. Not surprisingly, many of these actions overlap.

Clear job descriptions for new hires. Employee loyalty can begin or end at the time of hire. Have you read your requisitions recently? I realize that we frequently work with legal documents, but when did we begin to use legalese when writing job postings? If an average, non-industry person cannot easily understand what the job entails, it should not be posted.

Another common mistake hiring managers make (on purpose or not) is in presenting an opportunity in a way that is difficult to turn down. It is one of those great "anything you want to make out of it" opportunities. Your employees will remember the promises you made and will expect them to come to fruition within a reasonable period of time. If they do not, you will have a dissatisfied employee and soon may need to fill that position again.

Career path for existing employees. Do any of the following situations sound like banking industry trends?

- Pressure to grow sales and earnings with the same or shrinking staff.
- Loss of valuable employees.
- No replacement of employees who left and spreading the work among remaining employees.
- Budget cuts in training.
- Executive compensation growth while employees face salary freezes.
- The erosion of employees' morale.

Surprisingly, the main concern of young professionals is not listed above. Younger generations are most concerned about being stuck in their current positions without clear learning and growth opportunities.

We all get caught up in our daily routines. When the entire organization loses perspective on what's important to a generation of employees, this is a guaranteed way to send them looking for new jobs.

Growth within the organization. Banks generally fail to open doors to internal growth. In a large financial outfit, chances are that employees in one group do not know what other groups are doing, who the key people are, and what career opportunities are available.

Smaller banks have a different set of developmental challenges for young professionals. They have small departments and limited growth opportunities. As a result, a junior to mid-career banker may be stuck in a role that does not change for many years and does not offer growth and advancement. As smaller banks typically do not have internal training programs and have been cutting their training budgets just like their large competitors, young bankers find themselves in the same routine year after year. This is what sends them packing.

Investment in employee training. Almost all of the survey respondents were disconcerted by the reduction in—or, in some cases, complete elimination of—training, be it initial or ongoing. This is viewed as a direct threat to young professionals' advancement simply because on-the-job training and mentorship are, at best, limited. Meanwhile, more and more banks opt to seek out external candidates rather than invest in their existing employees. It is a trade-off between an immediate solution to a problem, which in the long run leads to the lack of loyalty and ultimately to young professionals' exodus. This is a prime example of "penny wise, pound foolish."

Providing challenge. Banks that assume "challenging" an employee means loading on an ever-mounting volume of work are missing the mark badly. Of course, every company wants to use its employees to best advantage. However, truly taking advantage of their full potential can only be achieved by developing your employees' strengths, talents, and interests.

Hearing the employee. Many banks invest significant resources in employee satisfaction surveys and other tools designed to find out what employees want and think. Then, not much happens. Senior managers may not agree with that assessment. However, ask your employees, and you will be unpleasantly surprised by the answers. Young professionals in particular are more than willing to share their concerns and suggestions on how to help them bring maximum benefit to their banks. The information is there and readily available. Why waste money on surveys if you don't take advantage of the information you glean from them?

Type casting. Many young professionals, including myself, have experienced the unpleasant industry phenomenon of being labeled. Once you have expertise in a certain area, it seems that

many banks want to use you only in that particular capacity and other doors close. For example, while I am a big proponent of small businesses, I currently prefer to work in lending to upper-tier small businesses and middle-market companies. My small-business advocacy and education efforts are done on my free time. However, I am often asked whether I am in the right place and why I am not doing small-business lending. Like everyone else, young professionals have various interests and want diverse experiences that will allow them to maximize their career opportunities. Give them a chance! You can invest lots of time into looking for a perfect candidate with varying degrees of success, or you can give internal candidates a chance to learn something new and have new high-achievers on your team. I once applied for an asset-based lending position, and I was told that I had not done that type of lending before. Well, *of course* I hadn't. If I had, why would I be applying for the same kind of position again?

Change the Status Quo

To hit—not miss—the mark, here are some approaches to doing better at retaining and taking full advantage of new generations of bankers.

Open culture and communication. Each organization has its own culture. However, a culture that excludes some employees is not a healthy one. I've seen this first hand, having worked in a group where a few senior colleagues guarded and preserved what they called "culture," which

was nothing more than poor interpretation of the company's overall environment. This so-called culture was inflexible, exclusive, and did not change with the times. Many younger generations of bankers find themselves in similar situations. Make them a part of the team. Let your culture evolve with time, let it be flexible, and let it be a reflection of each person's values.

Transparency, transparency, and transparency. Help your employees understand their job responsibilities and career options. If your bank is large, provide information on various departments, the career paths that exist there, and who can help the employee learn more about them. Place all this information on the intranet and keep it updated. It is in your interest to help your young professionals learn about your organization's structure instead of causing them to move blindly between departments or leave the bank altogether. It is also important for junior to mid-

Let your culture evolve with time, let it be flexible, and let it be a reflection of each person's values.

level bankers to see the big picture and the results of their work, as it is the best way to motivate your employees. For example, encourage them to participate in higher-level meetings or in meetings with customers. Take advantage of your employees' true strengths, talents, and interests. This will translate into an improving bottom line for your company.

Mentorship programs and rotations. Mentorship programs cannot be a superficial and occasional effort. They should be consistent to allow tenured bankers to pass on their knowledge and professional wisdom. This builds continuity in your business units and brings up new generations of well-trained, loyal employees. It is not as difficult as some may think to create a culture that fosters mentorship and collaboration. However, it has to be encouraged consistently—for several months and even several years—before it becomes second nature. Make mentorship projects a category in the evaluation forms of every employee above entry level.

Rotations to explore new opportunities within the bank are another traditionally weak area for banks. Some banks do offer rotations, or cross-training, but only at the start of an employee's career. Opportunities to develop a

diverse set of skills do not last long. I realize that business needs are important, but your banking organization and its customers will not be served well by employees who can't wait to get out. Rotations need not be long and disruptive. Assess how many days it takes to look for a new employee and provide training until he or she can fulfill the requirements of the job. Isn't it advantageous to create your own internal pipeline?

An example of a company that encourages its employees to grow comes from outside our industry. I was pleasantly surprised when my wife's employer, Genzyme—and her supervisor in particular—were supportive of her interest in exploring another department within the company. She was invited to join several meetings and was able to spend an occasional day or two over a span of a few weeks with that department. In exchange for a four- or five-day rotation, the company retained an employee who is even more dedicated.

"Investment" is not a four-letter word. Articles have been written concerning the true costs of losing an employee and hiring a new one, frequently from outside the company and at a higher salary.[1] These costs include a company's reputation, as employees

who leave out of frustration are unlikely to espouse the virtues of working for your bank. Nor will your customers appreciate having someone new foisted on their account. A current employee requires just a few hours and a modest investment to help him or her become more proficient. The alternative is to spend hours interviewing prospects and bringing the new hire up to speed without the guarantee of success. Yes, some employees may leave your organization after having received training, but a greater number will certainly leave it if they don't.

Promotions. Are promotions to management guided mostly by the number of years people have been in banking rather than by managerial successes? Younger generations of bankers need good managers—whether they have clocked in the years or not—because the onset of their careers is when they most need guidance and may be most receptive to coaching.

Always know why your employees are leaving. Last but not least, learn why your employees are leaving and fix the problems. If you choose not to fix them, at least determine the true costs and risks of not doing so. Word travels fast, and prospective employees will stay away from your bank. I know at least three commercial banks in the greater Boston area that I will not work for no matter how lucrative the opportunity. In my experience, young professionals tend to be particularly proactive in sharing their thoughts about banks with which they have had a bad experience. So don't be surprised if you are unable to attract qualified candi-

> I truly believe that it is possible to create a better growth environment for employees and that happy employees result in satisfied customers' profitable performance.

dates after you have disappointed some of your junior to mid-career employees.

Conclusion

Banking products and services have become a commodity. We ourselves have taught our customers to focus on pricing and, as a result, now suffer from customers jumping from bank to bank in search of the cheapest deal. I think we have done the same to employees' attitudes. At some point, we began treating our human assets as a commodity—everybody is dispensable if the earnings game warrants it. Thus, it does not surprise me that employees' morale and loyalty have sunk to new lows.

It is hard for me to believe that I loathed my first two or three years in commercial lending. I particularly disliked how far behind financial services seemed to be in offering all employees a rewarding career path. Fortunately for me, I found my place in the industry, and I absolutely love the opportunities it offers. Unfortunately, not many younger bankers share that sentiment.

I have been hearing that more and more organizations have begun to focus on retaining their customers. I suspect that the lack of focus on employee retention and growing attrition will become a great problem in the next five to 10 years, if it is not already a threat to the financial well-being of some banks.

I truly believe that it is possible to create a better growth environment for employees and that happy employees result in satisfied customers' profitable performance. In addition, I truly hope this article spurs debates and, most important, actions that will benefit all our employees and ultimately our customers. ❑

Contact Dima Berdiev by e-mail at DBerdiev@bostonprivatebank.com; more information on his book is available at www.LoanFinancingGuide.com. Berdiev thanks all the people—bankers and nonbankers—who took their time to share their thoughts and concerns.

Notes
1 For examples, visit the following sites:
• www.clomedia.com
• www.incentivecentral.org/The_Economics _of_Retention.553.0.html#2
• www.retainsemployees.com/new_hire_ article.pdf
• www.enewsbuilder.net/peoplereport/e_ article000617464.cfm?x=b7HNfOG,b55mLThT,w

To respond to this article, e-mail Beverly Foster at bfoster@rmahq.org; include in your response whether or not the Journal *may publish your comments.*

CHAPTER IV – ARE YOU WILLING TO PUT IN AN EFFORT TO EARN YOUR PLACE?

When talking about earning *your* place in your company, in the industry, within your network, and with your customers, whether internal or external, I would divide the "earning" into two parts:

i) Earning your place in general as part of earning your stripes (a.k.a. paying your dues), and

ii) Earning your place as part of your specific career plan in your current position, organization and beyond.

In both cases, the vast majority of us have to earn that place, and it will not be handed to us on a silver platter. I hope that by now you are asking what I mean by "earning" and "place."

Earning

"Earning" is a concept that is not clearly defined and varies from industry to industry. It changes from time to time as the expectations of people change and society continues to evolve. A very basic example could be "working long hours" as the way to earn good standing and your place in your company. If you prefer a better work – non-work balance or for other reasons do not want to work the hours expected, that is a disconnect in the values that you are guided by versus the values and expectations of your company. A typical solution could be to find a new organization that requires fewer hours (especially if the compensation is the same), changing your values if the organization and/or industry you are in is where you want to and should be, or potentially leaning on your trust fund and doing nothing (for those few who have them).

Place

Place ultimately means the right to stay and be employed (at a minimum) as well as the right to learn, develop, grow, be compensated well, advance and be successful (whatever your definition of success is).

Your action plan, in its simplest sense, should be:

a) To understand what the expectations are for earning your place within your organization and your industry;

b) To decide how that compares to what you would like to do and your personal values and interests; and

c) To make a commitment to do what's needed to earn your stay AND actually do it.

The Big Disconnect I have observed in the commercial banking industry is the generational misunderstanding between what more tenured and perhaps older generations feel it means to earn your stay and what newer, typically younger generations think it means. Here are just a couple of the numerous examples I have experienced over the years.

Example #1: You are an intern at a commercial bank. Although intern jobs can and often are less defined than regular jobs, you can add considerable value if you have the drive, industriousness and desire to get things done and make a positive impression. Granted, you must not expect that you will be doing something glamorous (if it happens, then it is a bonus but do not have high expectations). Let's say you come in at 8:30, take your allotted lunch at 12:00 and leave on the dot at 5:00 pm. You also do not seem to have a sense of urgency to get through your backlog, even when there is little else to do. Furthermore, you never raise your hand to ask for more work when you are done with your assignment (if you do, you sit around and wait for a while until you are completely bored) and do not ask for more to challenge yourself and show that you are eager to get the job done.

Example #2: You are a credit analyst who is doing fine overall. Similarly to the above example, you clock in and clock out at regular times and not much more. You get your job done fine and overall are meeting expectations. What you do not realize is that the expectations are, at bare minimum, to perform adequately and to be in good standing. When you come to your manager asking for a raise or talk about wanting to grow and advance, your actions have been conveying the opposite message, and you are surprised that your employer does not see you as a high potential employee.

Using the examples above, it is a good time to share with you what I have heard from my more senior colleagues over years of work in commercial banking and why they think this way. Note that this is a general opinion and perhaps a stereotype, which does not describe everybody in your generation. What's more important is to see this as an opportunity for you to stand out from the crowd, if you are willing to take advantage of this information. The general opinion is that the younger generations want it all, including growing salaries and titles (not necessarily responsibilities), but do not want to put an effort into their work and expect advancement while working limited hours and having a good balance of work and non-work life. By effort I mean both a good effort to produce acceptable results as well as an extra effort, if you want to do better than your peers.

Why do older and more tenured generations want to see you work hard, at least sometimes longer and more unorthodox hours, to do everything possible to get the job done, and have more commitment and passion for what you do? The answer is simple. This expectation is based on their personal experiences, how they had to work to get where they are now, and what was expected from them. I am not discussing if it is right or wrong. You can fight or accept this view, but you will not be able to change it until you have achieved something and are in a position of authority. And, quite frankly, chances are when you achieve growth, a higher position, more responsibilities and higher compensation, you may expect similar behaviors of up and coming generations of employees because that's what it took you to advance. An unfortunate fact that I have to note is that your senior colleagues may not be good at providing feedback and coaching you on what it means to be successful. As a consequence, they will not communicate the above information directly, clearly and professionally. Thus, take notes now.

If you look at older generations of bankers, you may say that you see lenders who are barely in the office and most of the time just sit around without doing much or spend their time on the golf course. So, why should you work hard, if all these individuals might not have had to work hard to get where they are now? Well, they probably did have to do all of the above to earn their place in banking. Additionally, even if there are some characters who just bounced along and eventually scored a cushy job that does not require much work, are you going to interview people to get to the bottom of it? What if you find out that it is true and their career paths were relatively easy? Will you go on strike or file a formal complaint? Will it change anything about your career and the expectations of you? Probably not. If anything, you will make a few enemies and show others that you want a free ride. Do not get caught up in this what about him or her "game"! Your career is about you and what you offer. By focusing too much on others, you are saying that you are not mature enough to do what you need to do to make your career thrive.

You will need to pay your dues to earn your place in your organization and in the industry and that may take time, as learning and development does not happen overnight. Sometimes it may take years and each time you change jobs and organizations you will again have to earn your place. The best way to approach this is to recognize it is as a reality of life and make this approach a part of your DNA, no matter how long you have been in your current role and overall career. Also accept that your more tenured colleagues and managers will have their own expectations, both individual and generational. Learn them, decide if you want to function within those boundaries, and work hard to meet and exceed those expectations, before you try to change the reality. And if you want to be successful in your professional career, I encourage you to write down this question as one of your guiding principles – what have you done in your role to make your organization materially competitive?

In conclusion, here are a few examples of what some credit managers will define as efforts:

- Efforts to meet your goals, whether quantitative or qualitative.

- Efforts to listen, take feedback and apply that feedback.

- Efforts to learn and apply that learning on the job.

- The longevity of your effort.

- Effort to put in terms of hours of work (unless you can complete your workload within business hours and meet or better yet exceed expectations).

- Effort to retain your earned level and build on it (i.e. continuous progress).

Ultimately, as I will discuss in more detail later in the book, efforts to achieve something are fantastic and that's where everything begins. However, after a while, if there are no results, efforts are no longer sufficient. If you had great parents, they probably constantly encouraged you to try hard, learn, improve, and do better. This was their way to teach you and prepare you for the harsh realities of the world – results are ultimately the name of the game!

CHAPTER V – BE SMART, KNOW YOUR OPTIONS AND HAVE A STRATEGY, A LONG-TERM ONE

It is to be expected that in the earlier years of your career you will have less of a vision of what you want to do. Your initial focus will be on learning as much as you can and trying to pay your bills, especially for those of you with large student loans and who live in expensive (urban) areas. As you gain more and more experience and begin to showcase your talents, begin developing that long-term, sustainable plan for how you would like your career to unfold. I am not suggesting that you write out your entire life. That's just not possible. What's important is to have a direction from which you build goals and work toward achieving them. To be honest, throughout your life you will go through phases when your career will find itself at a crossroads. This is normal.

A longer term plan is paramount in ensuring that you do not bounce from job to job aimlessly. Granted, it will not be easy to think long term because we are absolutely surrounded by a widespread obsession with nearsighted focus on what's going to happen in the next few months or quarters. We see it on Wall Street with the many publicly traded companies that have traded long-term vision for short-term, quarter-to-quarter outlook that has been shown to be myopic and unsustainable. The same is true for politicians who live from one round of election day promises to the next rather than having a sustainable and well-balanced plan to represent those that they were elected to represent. This is your opportunity to learn from their mistakes, which clearly show how a short-term focus leads to a one of a kind recession (among other economic issues) and a government that is just falling apart. If you set your attention on the next few months at a time or that next job without seeing the bigger picture, you risk taking jobs that are not in the best interest of your career and are instead a detour from what you'd want to be a learning experience leading to growth opportunities.

My strong recommendation is to think of your career as similar to what we encourage and quite frankly expect our borrowers to do – invest in their long term on a regular basis, producing assets, also known as capital expenditures (CAPEX). CAPEX could mean investment in long-lasting assets such as equipment, facilities, intellectual property or human capital assets. What are your capital assets as an individual? The list includes your education, your professional training, the skills that are of value to your employer and the industry, your experiences, your expertise and know-how, your drive and energy, and even your reputation and your network. These are your longer lifecycle assets that can produce results for your benefit and for the benefit of others.

How do you keep those assets working and producing? You need to use them on a regular basis and try to take the most advantage of them. For instance, if your skill is research, use it and perfect it when working on financing requests. Also constantly hone those skills. In the same example, you can improve your ability to sift through information faster and achieve the same results. Don't forget to invest or reinvest in this research "capital asset." It can be accomplished by taking additional courses, self study or even seeking coaching and advice from experts in your network on how you can broaden and better apply your research skills. I think you get the message: a) use them regularly and take the most advantage of them; b) hone, improve and perfect those skills; and c) invest additional resources to substantially upgrade your skills periodically. As noted by a very smart (but unknown to me) person, "do it as if you have a lifetime to do yet today is your last day."

There are very many opportunities and directions your career can take within banking. These options can be overwhelming if you do not know what you want to do or when you want to do too many different things at the same time. You should always keep an inventory of opportunities and options and update it. For example, do you know the landscape of professional opportunities and career tracks that exist within your industry and your region? Do you know how many organizations there are in your state or region, what career paths exist for a person of your background, how those organizations are doing, what their strengths and weaknesses are, and the overall direction of the industry? If not, it is time to get back to the drawing board, start reading and researching. I sure hope that you will start with your organization first. Like the fact that it takes a lot more time and expense to bring a new client into a bank than to retain one, it is takes a lot more time, effort and to some extent money (as it converts to your compensation) to switch organizations. Try to figure out if you can find a better place and career track where you are. As suggested by the CEO of Brookline BanCorp, Inc., Paul Perrault, who spoke at a Risk Management Association New England Chapter event in 2011: "Presume that you will be in your job forever. And this does not mean being comfortable in what you do and having a sleepy, cushy job. I refer to making it a goal to learn everything you possibly can, doing the best you can, and people will notice you."

Once you have a plan that offers a possible direction and indicates the skills and experiences you will need to gain, don't jump at the first sight of opportunity that comes your way. Make every move count. Make sure that each move is in the interest of your long term career and offers the learning and training you desire. As an example, if you know the overall banking landscape, there is a tremendous shortage of credit analysts with 2-5 years of experience for reasons that are beyond the scope of this book. This should tell you that there are opportunities and perhaps quite a few to choose from. Certainly this is true in urban areas such as Boston. On the other hand, make sure that you are not too picky. Do you want every job to be your most perfect job? Well, there is no such thing. Essentially any job has mundane elements to it as well as a production component, conflicts, office politics and other challenges. There is nothing wrong with seeking a career path that gives you satisfaction and makes you want to wake up in the morning to go to work. This should be a goal. However, there may be a few steps before you reach it. Just focus on what you would really want to do and what you need to do to get there.

Now, a couple of words on what it means to have not just a long-term career view but also a sustainable one. By one of many definitions (in this case, www.merriam-webster.com), "sustainable" refers to using a resource so it is not depleted or permanently damaged. In the case of a career plan, "sustainable" in my view means maintaining a patient balance between learning, development, growth and compensation, and following the path you have chosen. Team attitude of a credit team I had an opportunity to run is one example of sustainability. Since the bank was growing and analysts were leaving to move to other banks after having worked there for a few years, the bank ended up hiring better-quality credit analysts. Management was quick to recognize the team as "the best team we have ever had." However, this recognition had a negative impact that came to the surface when I took over the team. All of the analysts across the board knew loud and clear that they were the best team the bank had ever had. This would not have been a problem but unfortunately the team decided to rest on its laurels and put no effort into personal or team growth. Very quickly the team's performance began to slip, even from the level it had been recognized for. This is a good example of how a positive comment made to encourage continuous improvement had an opposite effect. The analysts did not realize that a) management did not mean that everybody on the team was a better analyst than before, and b) being the best required ongoing improvements rather than kicking back and relaxing.

CHAPTER VI – YOUR NETWORK IS YOUR GROWTH FUEL

Networking as a concept has been defined for many years and there are dozens of books and articles written on the subject. Yet, many of us miss the very fundamental best practices of networking, such as the following:

- Your network, just like your reputation, takes a lifetime to develop and a day to lose;

- The quality of your network is comparable to quality of credit analysis – garbage in, garbage out;

- Networking is first and foremost less about you and more about other people and how you can be of value to them;

- You can choose to play the numbers game when it comes to networking, but that is not the same as quality. Quality and quantity do not usually go well together;

- If you cannot make your net work for you, there is no point in having one.

As you are more junior in your career, it is to be expected that your network will be limited at first, but it should grow over time if you put the right amount of effort into it. Your network should encompass various groups of people, including but not limited to your former and current classmates, former and current colleagues (peers who are more senior, and more junior as you grow), former and current bosses, various direct and indirect business partners, customers, family and friends, social networks, and people who are not currently in your network but who you can easily reach through your networks or directly. One of the greatest misconceptions among or about credit analysts is that because you are a credit professional you should not and will not have a strong network. The same unfounded and misguided opinions exist for those who are more on the risk management or other analytical tracks in their careers. Why shouldn't you have a network, even if you are not a sales professional? Some may say that networks are for business developers to bring business. It is certainly true that business developers rely heavily on their networks to help generate sales but to say that you have no need for a network that is just as strong because you are in an analytical line of business is to have no understanding of the purpose of networks.

Here is a short list, not an all-inclusive one, of why you need networks regardless of your career tracks.

- Networks are there for all of us to make desired career moves: to grow, be successful, and hopefully happy in what we do.

- Networks are a valuable source of learning and development as well as a resource in solving our daily work challenges.

- Networks are important in coaching, mentoring and educating yourself and others.

- Your career goals, aspirations, and actual careers change from time to time and what was of no interest yesterday could be a new goal tomorrow. Your network can help in this major undertaking.

An important question that comes up all the time is the quality of your network as well as its extensiveness. *Quality* can be defined as the strength of your relationship with network members, which will determine their desire to assist you; the quality of those individuals in terms of their experience, rank in their companies and industries; the ethical foundation of your network members; and, finally, the usefulness of your network when you need its assistance. The *extensiveness* of your network is defined by the number of individuals in your network as well as the number of individuals you can reach fairly easily if you need to, which one way or another ties back into quality or the lack thereof. There is a symbolic yin – yang relationship (the symbol is below) for those who are familiar with this Eastern philosophical concept (the extreme opposite nature of quality and quantity of your network that are polar opposites yet are interdependent, intertwined and give rise to each other).

While quality and quantity are not mutually exclusive, there needs to be a balance between the two. Having too few very useful network members will limit your options, while too many network members that you have no relationship with means it is unlikely they will give you a helping hand when assistance is needed.

In the age of social networks (both personal and professional), we are increasingly detached from our network members. We focus on growing networks by increasing numbers but quality is concentrated in posting trivial updates that people for the most part do not care about. There is certainly little reason to care because chances are you do not know those individuals. Here is a little challenge. Look through your LinkedIn and other network base and answer the following questions on a scale from 1 (no / very little) to 5 (yes / highly). If your average score is 2 or less, your network is primarily transactional and not based on relationships.

- Have you worked with this individual and can you attest to his/her industriousness, technical skills and other professional qualities?

- Can you say that you know this network member well?

- How familiar are you with the ethical qualities of this network member and do you have trust and confidence in this individual?

- How well are these individuals familiar with you?

- How likely would these individuals be to act as your resource, invest their time and efforts in you and extend a helping hand to you?

- How likely are you to be a resource to everybody in your network, investing your time and efforts and extending a helping hand to them?

The larger your network, the more likely your average score to be 2 or lower. This is especially common in this day and age when online networks have become a numbers game of growing your network in numbers but with little real connection to members in those networks. As a result of this numbers chase, we forget about the true meaning of the word "network." To see and avoid the common mistakes made by many individuals in networking for business-related purposes, read the article after this chapter.

How long does it take to develop a quality network? It all depends on why you need the network. To truly establish some connection with people and grow the circle to a meaningful number takes a bit of time. If you need your network today to explore career opportunities, solve a professional challenge, or grow in your industry (among other motivations for needing that outside assistance), you are too late. Depending on why you need your network's assistance and resourcefulness, it may take from several weeks to several months to identify the individuals you want to connect with, build some sort of a bond and relationship with them, get to know your network prospects, find out how you can be of value to them, and actually engage the network to help you achieve your goals.

Suffice it to say that most of my significant learning experiences, professional development and growth, and actual jobs came through my network. One important question to ask yourself is how you can pay forward to your network members and how you can potentially offer value to them. While it may not be possible with everyone in your network, this kind of thought process can have an enormous positive impact on relationship with your network. I recently met with an individual who is much more senior than I am in terms of experience and accomplishments. As our conversation progressed, he must have taken a liking of me and felt that he'd be interested in allowing me into his network. He welcomed me into his network by offering several valuable introductions that would enhance my growth and learning.

Also ask yourself whether and how much your track-record can impress your network members now, before you need their assistance and support. Right now and every single moment is the time to do outstanding, high quality job and demonstrate positive attitude so that your reputation precedes you within your network. People remember that, especially when you may need to call on them. Last but not least, if you are just networking for the purposes of getting jobs, you have missed the whole point about networking and having a quality network. Jobs come and go. Expertise, career tracks, and relationships with people is what leads to true learning, development and growth! Make your net work for you!

CHAPTER VII – LEARNING FROM THE BEST – ONLINE NETWORKING ESSENTIALS FOR THE 21ST CENTURY

Online professional networking has evolved to become a powerful tool for growing and managing one's network. The days of Rolodexes and Outlook Contacts may be numbered, but you should not rush into discounting them as old school and ineffective. Why? The maturity levels and evolution of users of sites like LinkedIn is far from where it should be, from a high-quality, professional networking point of view. As the saying goes, "don't put anything in an email that you would not put in a letter." Similarly, don't get into networking unless you are prepared to do it with the highest spirit of professionalism, communication, and business relationship. In other words, use online networking tools as if you were networking in person.

What are the common mistakes of online networking?

First and foremost, for many individuals online networking is a numbers game and a chase to secure growth in the number of network members rather than developing quality, functional relationships. The result is large networks that do not work and do not produce ultimate results – they lack member engagement, the knowledge or familiarity of members with each other is scant, and relationships with them are also lacking. How is this different from not having any network at all? When you need to get your "net working" (the first time I have heard this term was during a marketing training by Richard Weylman), you will still need to go through the challenges of getting to know people and letting them get to know you. This takes time, as people are not invested in helping you if they do not know and respect you, and therefore have an incentive to help you.

There are also a number of "don'ts" that are common sense and, if you understand them, you can establish a network that can truly function to your benefit, whether you need it to generate new business, help you in your career growth, or achieve other goals.

Don'ts

- Do not drop people impersonal or "built-in" standard invitation messages asking them to join your network, particularly people you actually know now, once knew, or have not communicated with in a while. If you do, what does it tell the other person? It says that you are too lazy to take a couple of seconds to type a personal message, and this is the kind of quality network member you are. It also says that you like spamming people with generic messages and do not care about maintaining a relationship.

- Do not send invitation messages to people whom you see regularly, without giving them advance notice, preferably in person when you next see them. If you do, what does it tell the other person? It says that you do not respect him or her enough or have the maturity to give the person a heads up that you are sending an invitation. The mere checklist of adding that person to your online network list is more important than the fact that you already know that individual.

- Do not underestimate the simple courtesy of asking if a person would like to join your network or if you can join his/hers. If you do, what does it tell the other person? It says that you do not have the simple consideration and respect to check if that individual is interested in connecting with you and that you think everybody uses this networking tool in the same shallow way.

- Do not provide recommendations to people and then ask them to do the same. If you do, what does it tell the other person? That there is something wrong with your ethical standards, and that he/she should not take any kind of recommendation from you seriously. Recommendations must be professional and appropriate, without any quid pro quo principle involved. Otherwise, they are meaningless, likely subjective and will not be taken seriously by others.

Just to demonstrate some of my points, here are a couple of recent examples.

- A former colleague of mine, whom I see very often and whom I always considered to be a part of my network, sends me an impersonal, standard invitation message without giving me heads up in person (preferred) or by email. This tells me that that individual does not even respect me enough to ask if that's okay, and perhaps he is flat-out lazy. Regardless of the reason, I do not ever want to have such a person in my network.

- A non-business acquaintance of mine dropped me an impersonal, standard request to join my network without asking if I was interested. If he had, I would have told him that I do not mix my personal and professional lives and only add to my professional network people I have done business with or know fairly well professionally. This rule would have excluded him from joining my business network but would have given him credibility to possibly be added in the future.

- A former acquaintance of mine, whom I barely knew, wrote a glowing recommendation for me and then immediately asked me to write one for her. How can this be taken seriously and where is the objectivity in this quid pro quo approach?

Remember that the present is a well-forgotten past – the well-established rules for proper networking etiquette are still as valid as they were 50 years ago, despite the new technology surrounding us. There is something to be said about professionalism and tact in networking, especially in our impersonal, online-based world. The chase after networking numbers may be exciting for a little while, but it does not create quality business relationships. You should balance quantity with quality and treat your network members as your business partners, not as numbers in a long list of blind hits. People are barraged with information every day, and there is a longing for a genuine relationship with the network. The numbers game in networking is a fad that will pass. When that happens, do not be left with a large but useless list of contacts. Happy networking!

PART IV –
HOW BADLY DO YOU WANT IT?

CHAPTER I – THE SKY'S THE LIMIT BUT BEING REALISTIC DOES NOT HURT

"The sky's the limit" is of course a figurative expression. Nonetheless, looking at all of my successes and failures, as well as those of other people, the phrase holds true for the vast majority of jobs as well as career tracks out there, not just in banking. What makes our times even more special in commercial banking is that technological, societal (increasing customer and employee turnover, and disappearing customer, employee and employer loyalty), competitive, and many other pressures are rushing like floodwaters of change into our industry. For those of you who view life with a negative and pessimistic attitude of a glass half empty, these changes, which I would characterize as turmoil, promise nothing good – lots of confusion, frustration, and struggle to learn and advance. For those of you who look at life and your professional environment as a glass half full, uncertainty and change will bring a vast array of opportunities. The key is to be entrepreneurial to recognize those opportunities, make quick and comprehensive assessments about which ones are right for you, and jump on those opportunities with focus and hard work in order to take full advantage of them.

An important part of capitalizing on opportunities that come your way is a very fine balance of setting your goals and dreams very high, yet being realistic about what you can and cannot do and what your current situation will allow you to do. You should weave into your understanding of "being realistic" what you learn in this book – the importance of paying your dues, the willingness to put in your time, the ability to put in effort and produce results, and the patience not to expect results overnight.

As an example, I will describe one of my best friends (let's call him Nick). Nick was always a very driven, hardworking, and intelligent person with a little touch of romanticism, naiveté and altruism. As long as I have known Nick, he has been determined to have a high-growth career with high earning potential and to do something he was very passionate about – making a difference in people's lives. This immediately sounds like a stretch, doesn't it? And he wanted to find all these qualities in his very first job. Thus, whenever he found a job in a new industry, he would expect his list of requirements to come true. Unfortunately, only a few of us have the luck and luxury of getting jobs that meet all our demands right away and show great income promise. Very quickly Nick would get frustrated with the jobs he got for a variety of reasons – he found them to be menial, low paying, he had little decision-making power, he wasn't making a difference in people's lives, and he didn't have enough patience to endure the routine. As a result, he switched through a number of jobs, companies and industries in the first ten to fifteen years of his professional life, without really finding a place where he was happy and that was the perfect fit for him. Part of his challenge was the inability to realize that the perfect place he dreamed of did not exist in real life but that a fancy, high-powered career is something that can be created. It takes time and perseverance, but it can be done. Nick was just not realistic enough to see the big picture and have the long-term vision and patience to get where he needed.

However, what always fascinated me in Nick was his industriousness in anything he did. He had and continues to have this incredible ability to get into a new job and a new career with a resume that is full of holes big enough to drain pasta, yet still land on his feet. One of his more recent gigs was a fairly low-level sales job at a high-end, organic and free-range produce distributor. Especially for the first few months, he worked practically day and night to learn the industry, understand what his company did and what was important to his customers, and build very strong relationships within his company and beyond. This earned him such an outstanding reputation with the management of this fast-growing organization that in just a little over a year he was promoted to manager of an entire region. I still do not know that many individuals who would fall hard and them pick themselves up, dust themselves off, and in the end without any prior experience become so successful. Unless you are just like Nick and have the endurance of a camel with a never-ending beam of hope, set your goals high but be realistic as you reach for them. Even if you are like Nick, having a realistic plan will allow you to avoid wasting time, build a professional path that is much more focused and will lead to a successful outcome without spending a decade or two tinkering around.

Applying the above to the path of the credit analyst, do you really want to be doing what you are doing? For some of you, being a credit analyst is just the means to an end and your ultimate goals will go beyond this job. If that's the case, I can see how you might not want to spend a day more than you have to being in credit analysis. However, you need to know how important this particular step is to your future roles. If you want to do anything with credit, risk management, lending, sales, or general management in commercial banking, credit is the very foundation that can make or break your banking journey. Do you think it is coincidental that so many different career paths in commercial banking start with becoming a good quality credit or financial analyst? Now that credit training programs are disappearing, credit analysts are ever more in demand. As an example, lenders who have skipped or just glossed over this important step are finding themselves outcompeted by their peers who are grounded in credit. Not every field has this universal foundation that can promise you a more successful advancement with solid credit training and experience. Some may view it as a limitation of commercial banking. I view it as a benefit. To me it brings a lot more clarity and differentiates those who have the foundation necessary to be successful from those who do not.

This brings us to an important point – even if the role of a credit or financial analyst is just one step in your career, make it count! It is one step that has to be done thoroughly to have a long-lasing ripple effect. If you try to find shortcuts and bypass the essential training and practical experiences that cement credit training over a number of years, your colleagues who make decisions about your advancements will figure it out quickly. If you hate credit and just want to do the bare minimum to qualify, your days will be extremely miserable, which is likely to poison the environment around you for other people. You will also signal to everyone that you may not have the maturity to stay focused to complete by far one of the most important steps of your banking development. This is hardly a way to establish yourself as a team player with a positive attitude and the ability to get the job done. Thus, the lesson in setting your goals high and the sky having no limit is based on doing well in everything you do, every step of the way.

I was recently speaking with one of my mentors. Let us call him Mack. Mack is a commercial lending executive in New York City. He was talking about a lender, his direct report (let's call him Jim). My mentor was having enormous difficulty working with Jim. Jim clearly rushed through his credit analyst training and very quickly landed a lending career. Now that he was becoming a senior lending team member, he was struggling more and more. When he would discuss a prospective lending opportunity, Mack would quickly discover that there was little support for Jim's prospects because he had missed some pretty clear and basic credit risks. He missed them because he did not learn the credit ropes of our job. Now that he was much more senior, it was tougher and tougher for Jim to admit what he did not know. It was also much more difficult for his bosses to send him back to the "credit school," especially since there is no quick fix for his shortcomings. It is tough to say what will happen in this situation, but I can predict that Jim will have serious roadblocks on the path of advancement, especially if he competes with a pool of lenders who have a strong credit foundation.

An important lesson of having no limit in where your career can take you can be borrowed from the world of real estate. If you talk to people who have rushed into deals, whether residential or commercial, they will tell you that there are always opportunities in the market. Similarly, if you are jumping on a career opportunity because someone (or perhaps circumstances) is whispering to you that this is the deal of a lifetime, you should know that, with very few exceptions, there are always great deals out there. A few years ago I saw my friends and customers jumping into buying sprees because they believed that the real estate market was so hot that there would be no other chance like it. About a year later when the collapse in the CMO markets in 2008 led to the residential real estate market meltdown with the rest of the economy to follow, they wished they had paused to think twice.

Around that same time, one customer of mine, a high-end residential real estate developer specializing in overhauling old buildings, saw the same incredible opportunity to buy a building for a seven figure price. He felt that while the opportunity was great, the run up in price was too fast and too high. Furthermore, there was too much pressure for the deal to close as soon as possible. His experience taught him that there were always opportunities, and he shrewdly and confidently walked away from the deal. A mere six months later, he had a chance to buy that same property for only a fraction of the price. He later joked that not rushing into the deal saved him $3 million or a half a million a month – not a bad return on patience!

Our career decisions seem to be clearer many years later. Do learn lessons from those career mistakes and successes. When I used to hear from my bosses that opportunities were limitless and could be anything I would make of them, I often felt disappointed. Part of my personal failure was that I was waiting for them to bring that next opportunity to me on a silver platter. Instead, I should have been fully committed and diving into my work to create opportunities for myself. For many years I did not realize one simple truth – we make our future today, every minute, every hour and every day. By not being present every moment I missed many opportunities that were slowly queuing in because I failed to show focus, commitment and patience in the present. So, if you want to fully experience how the sky can have no limits, dream big yet do not forget that endless opportunities are being created by excelling right now in very small, simple and, at times, menial tasks.

CHAPTER II – CREATING YOUR OWN OPPORTUNITIES

A small group of thoughtful people could change the world. Indeed, it's the only thing that ever has. Margaret Mead

Some of the smartest and most successful people I have met do not wait for opportunities to land at their feet – they create them! A big part of their success is seeing need and the opportunity today. That opportunity does not have to be anything fancy; usually it is not. As a matter of fact, some of the best opportunities are often less glamorous for most people to look at. And what those successful individuals do is not only notice them but also take advantage of them. This reminds me of my days in business school at Babson where the instructors, who were often accomplished entrepreneurs, kept our focus not on our great ideas and visions but on the problem of our prospective customers. "What is their pain or need?" we heard time and time again. Then, the next question was about who those customers were, followed by how our product or service would solve their pain or need. This is strikingly similar to what successful individuals do in their jobs on a daily basis.

Let's start with your role as a credit analyst. Ask yourself and perhaps your colleagues (team leader, lenders and others) about the key problems a credit analyst is there to address. This is the very basic reason for credit analysts to exist in the workplace. While those answers may vary from person to person, they will likely converge on the following points:

- Get as many deals done as possible to support the bank's business development efforts and help complete the sales loop (i.e. make the sale happen or close the deal).

- Get those deals done with the highest level of credit quality, yet balancing credit and business development needs as much as possible.

- Act in the capacity of a COO (Chief Operating Officer) to lenders in helping line up the various components of underwriting and the approval of a deal. Some may refer to this as being a highly proficient project manager for the lender by taking ownership in the deal.

- Maintain a very positive attitude when everybody is usually under the stress of timelines and juggling various deals at the same time. My current Chief Credit Officer calls it being a facilitator, which is not an easy task to accomplish. I would say that when you have the responsibility for being such an important element of approving a deal, yet typically do not have the authority, whether signing authority or otherwise, is one of the hardest (white collar) jobs there is. If you can be highly successful in this role, you can do almost any job out there.

I would also add to the list the following:

- Be entrepreneurial. For that, you do not have to start and run your own business. I have heard the term "corporate intrapreneur" that can define a highly successful credit analyst.

- Work toward specific, achievable and measurable results.

Let's spend a bit more time on the term "intrapreneur." As defined by the American Heritage Dictionary (quoted at www.intrapreneur.com), an intrapreneur is a person at a "large corporation who takes direct responsibility for turning an idea into a profitable finished product through assertive risk-taking and innovation." Intrapreneurship is the way of living for highly successful people in the corporate environment. Gifford Pinchot provides the Intrapreneur's Ten Commandments, which eloquently and precisely define the qualities that can and should guide a successful credit analyst-intrapreneur. From *Intrapreneuring, Why you don't need to leave the corporation to become an entrepreneur* by Gifford Pinchot III. President and Co-founder of Bainbridge Graduate Institute. Printed with permission.

I.   Come to work each day willing to be fired.

II.   Circumvent any orders aimed at stopping your dream.

III.   Do any job needed to make your project work, regardless of your job description.

IV.   Find people to help you.

V.   Follow your intuition about the people you choose, and work only with the best.

VI.   Work underground as long as you can – publicity triggers the corporate immune system.

VII.   Never bet on a race unless you are running in it.

VIII.   Remember, it is easier to ask for forgiveness than for permission.

IX.   Be true to your goals, but be realistic about the way to achieve them.

X.   Honor your sponsors.

What I would like to add to the above is a) make sure that all your actions are always highly ethical (ethics should never be compromised) and b) the corporate intrapreneurship of a credit analyst starts with the very small and basic tasks of your day-to-day work.

As you do your daily work, you need to make sure that you accomplish first and foremost the primary responsibilities the credit analyst job was created for, as I outlined above and as guided by your company. Then, when you are meeting and exceeding your primary goals, investigate daily problems and challenges. People in general tend to be used to those challenges and take them as part of unavoidable reality. They do not pause for a moment to decide how they can solve them. This is your opportunity to add value above and beyond your call of duty.

As an example, a fellow credit analyst was handed an incredible opportunity to do a project of bringing together credit and lending employees. The task at hand was to bring about quick improvements to the turnaround time of underwriting deals by solving the challenges that were quickest and easiest to address. We all know that there are many things we can do to be more efficient, and they do not require substantial changes. It is just a matter of pausing and reexamining our processes and behaviors. In this particular example, the analyst spent several months preparing the project and ultimately ended up convincing himself that nothing could be improved. In the process, he somehow managed to "convince" project participants that the undertaking was not worth the effort!

You may be wondering how this was possible. He approached this exercise with a very negative attitude. His focus was on what lenders could do differently rather than on organizing meetings and running them in the most constructive problem-solving fashion. As a result, this assignment was reassigned to another analyst who completed the project with a materially positive impact on the bank. This is an example of having an opportunity to make a difference and failing miserably simply because of not believing it possible. You may have seen the same situation in your organizations when people sit around the table pointing at one another and suggesting what others should do differently. The change, however, has to start within each one of us and finger-pointing does not lead to anything good.

A complete opposite example is that of an analyst on my team who would approach me with ideas of how to do things differently and often better. Not every idea would make sense to run with but this did not discourage him. He once approached me with an idea of outlining a set of common guidelines for analyzing the financial statements of guarantors of privately held companies. There have been many inconsistencies in how we as a bank have done our analysis, but nobody ever stopped to come up with ground rules that would help us work through deals faster, more effectively, and with an improved way of managing credit risk. He took the initiative, which led to noticeable improvements in our analytical tools and saved us all a good amount of time from that point onward. Nobody before him noticed this opportunity because it was not something glamorous. Yet, the impact on the team left a meaningful imprint and allowed this analyst to stand out as a valuable contributor to the team. Add to that the fact that he was performing well in his day-to-day responsibilities, and you have a powerful combination that can promise learning, development, and growth.

In conclusion, always remember that you are the one who can create opportunities for your career advancement. First and foremost, you need to excel in your day-to-day tasks and ensure that you meet the primary goals for your job to exist. Second, look at the low-hanging fruit type of improvements that can be made in your job or beyond and that would have a materially positive impact on your organization. If you identify such an improvement opportunity, try to see if you can lead the project but be open to sharing the opportunity with others or even having someone else run it. The goal is the positive impact and not turf wars. Third, remember to look at your day-to-day responsibilities, processes and challenges with a fresh pair of eyes. They may not be glamorous, yet they can offer an opportunity to make a difference in part because others are not seeing them in their daily routine and do not care for improvements to mundane challenges.

CHAPTER III – GOING ABOVE AND GOING BEYOND

Your time is limited, so don't waste it living someone else's life. Don't be trapped by dogma, which is living with the results of other people's thinking. Don't let the noise of others' opinions drown out your own inner voice, heart and intuition. They somehow already know what you truly want to become. Everything else is secondary. Steve Jobs, 2005, Stanford commencement speech

It is hard to not be inspired by the Steve Jobs' quote above. It is reinvigorating and can apply to various points of our lives and our careers. Earlier in our professional endeavors, when most of us have very basic jobs that can monotonous, this quote can help inspire us to be do-ers and to see the light at the end of the tunnel. As we become older and lose the inspiration of our earlier years, it can help rekindle the sprit that we often lose under the pressure of broken dreams and mortgages to pay.

As you are in your first years as a credit analyst, your greatest challenges will likely be in the realm of doing what may seem to be a very basic and unsophisticated job of crunching numbers, being the low person on the totem pole, being surrounded by colleagues who may not give you proper respect because in their eyes you have not yet achieved anything and they believe you are there to make sure that their business runs smoothly. Overall, you are nobody, and it may seem at a first glance that your job does not have any value. This is when it may be the time to pause, look at the quote above, talk to your colleagues who have been in your shoes and have proven otherwise – there is an endless field of opportunities for you. The opportunities are open to those who can go above and beyond.

Going above and beyond should first and foremost mean mastering your trade at the highest possible level of quality. If you do not have credit analyst knowledge and skills wired into you as if they were your second nature, you will not be able to progress as a high quality credit professional. The second component of going above and beyond is delivering your very basic yet incredibly valuable services to the various customer groups in the spirit of customer service excellence. While an entry level, the job of a credit analyst, if done well, allows lenders to be productive and successful at brining, booking, and managing deals. These are very simple priorities that many of us, myself included, did not learn to appreciate for quite some time, and you should take advantage of this knowledge. You do not have to be a shark longing to get to the top of the corporate tank. Anybody and everybody can be very successful in his or her career by staying focused on these simple priorities. It also does not matter whether you want to spend your career in credit or not, because your next role will likely present an opportunity to excel in the very same or similar behaviors as the basis for opening growth opportunities. If you cannot focus here and now on going above and beyond, there is no reason for your employer or your team to think that you will be motivated to do so in another role.

Another common mistake is thinking that going above and beyond has to be done every minute, every hour, and every day. Naturally, if this is how you operate, you are already standing out from the pack as a superior performer. Nonetheless, even occasional examples of going beyond your call of duty can mean a world of difference in how your institution views you as a credit analyst and in consideration for future opportunities. I recall managing a former credit team. Analysts would typically arrive by about 8:30am and would leave by about 5pm. Many would perform within expectations in terms of how many deals they underwrote, with what level of quality and by meeting other requirements of the job. However, there were numerous opportunities for them to take on a bit more and get the recognition they sought. Unfortunately, the team almost never took advantage of these easy opportunities.

What they were not aware of is that management was always on the look-out for people to take on more and in return be rewarded with opportunities to grow. Yet, there was nobody to step up to the plate. It was absolutely obvious that the analysts were eager to grow their careers. A major disconnect was that they wanted recognition and chances to advance for what management saw as doing the bare minimum. What was even more frustrating to management is that on a number of occasions their behavior communicated what little effort was needed to be recognized for making an above and beyond effort. Still, there were no takers. Do not expect that you will be praised for just doing your job. This is not how the business world operates. You get paid for doing your job, and it is going above and beyond that gets rewarded with praise.

At some point the team hired an analyst who pretty quickly figured out what the rules of the game were, and he was naturally inclined to go above and beyond in his job. It did not take long for his efforts to pay off and results to be recognized. He was offered a promotion within a year of joining the team. I cannot describe the level of indignation from the team toward management (and the analyst himself) for promoting the person who was on the team for the shortest period of time. I was very quick to point out at a team meeting exactly what kinds of achievements led to the recognition. Alas, the team's conclusion was that the promotion was unfair. Be that as it may, I hope that you will be able to recognize similar simple, low-hanging fruit that constitutes going above and beyond that would in turn lead to above and beyond results. There is a saying: "you reap what you sow."

While I will always be the proponent of excelling in one's career every step of the way, I would like to give another example of at least occasionally going above the call of duty. Suppose you are an analyst on a credit team at a middle market lending unit who underwrites about one deal per week. After 3 weeks of vacation every year, you are left with 49 weeks a year when you can put your name on about 49 deals. Even without much of an effort, almost any analyst on his or her own accord can complete 10% more deals by working a bit smarter and by working the same hours every week. That 10% improvement will result in 5 more deals per year. To you this may seem like a small number but let's say each deal brings on average $10,000 in fee income to the bank. You now have helped the bank generate $50,000 in additional fee income! This accomplishment alone is largely an equivalent to your annual salary. This is before the interest income to the bank and income from deposits and other income streams.

Let's say the average loan size at your bank is $3,000,000. At an average interest rate of 4% and with only 50% of those balances outstanding, you have helped your bank generate $300,000 in annual interest income. Now, how about that for a contribution to the bottom line? And the beauty of this is that you have achieved it without breaking a sweat – just by working smarter, more efficiently, and being more focused. Imagine if your team consists of several analysts. The impact across the team can be tremendous. On my 1st credit team that I managed, we increased deal production over a team of 5 analysts by 33%. Think about the impact we had on the company's financial condition! This is quite an achievement to add to your list of accomplishments as an analyst.

It is true to say that people like Steve Jobs are born once in an era. Yet, we all can accomplish so much more by making a better effort in our daily work and by even occasionally going above and beyond. Everything begins with (or ends with) caring about your career and your future. What you have to realize is that everything is in your hands. I had an analyst on my team once who saw lenders, the underwriting process, and anybody and anything else but him as an obstacle to his ability to be successful on the job. It took an incredible effort and large amount of energy to be his manager, playing the role of his coach, his shrink, and his cheerleader daily. You will guess right if you suppose that he wasn't the first choice when growth opportunities came along. If anything, he was the last choice. Remarkably, it was not very difficult for him to do things better. All he needed to do is to look at things in a bit more positive light and just make effort his starting point. While he made some efforts to improve, these efforts were short-lived, and he would time and time again revert to his old ways. I hope that this chapter shows that going above and beyond is within reach for everybody, if you have the desire to be successful.

CHAPTER IV – FORGET WHAT THEY TOLD YOU – THEY LIED!

If you have gone through an educational institution in the U.S. for your undergraduate degree, especially the pricier, top-tier schools, chances are you have been brain washed into a belief that can hurt you once you are out in the real world of work. According to Academy Award winning director Davis Guggenheim's documentary, *Waiting for Superman*, our sense of (possibly unsubstantiated) confidence ranks us at the top of other countries. That's what happened to me and many others like me. I am not sure how the educational systems are in around the globe but I started my education in my home country of Turkmenistan and continued at a college in Vermont. Once I, along with a few of my compatriots, commenced our studies in the U.S., we very quickly learned that we were the best academically prepared individuals and that the world would be essentially at our feet when we graduate. Professors and college staff talked about the world of opportunities and possibilities and how we were positioned better than anybody else out there to succeed and grow upon graduation. Whether this was intended or not, we graduated on the wings of these inspirational speeches, completely exhilarated to conquer the world and make our mark on it.

And, what happens once you graduate? You fall on your face realizing a very painful truth – they lied! Once you are out, you will pretty quickly find out that besides a world of opportunities, there is also a world of hundreds of financial statement spreads and other rudimentary number crunching tasks, photocopying and many other basic job functions. While the energy to change the universe remains untapped within you, you must deal with slumlords and crummy apartments with ugly roommate wars, ramen or angel hair and Prego pasta sauce as your daily cuisine, living paycheck to paycheck and just making ends meet with a pile of college loans, along with everything else that is a stark difference to what they so energetically were instilling in you in school.

You may think that this is the most somber section of this book, and you are right. So, what is the point? Well, the point is to prepare you better for something I have seen individuals with many years of experience after graduation not getting on their own – how to function well and succeed in the work force. Understand that all these educational institutions are trying to achieve is to prove to you that you did not spend your money in vain (besides giving you the education proper). I can absolutely see how they have to be even more inspiring and motivational in this tough economy when I would not want to be a new graduate. I thought that times were tough in the 1990s, but my times were a piece of cake compared to what recent graduates face now. What all these educational establishments are trying to tell you is that the world is indeed filled with possibilities and opportunities but not with guarantees. What they forget to tell you in the process is that you are competing with thousands of equally intelligent, educated, and driven individuals who will work just as hard, if not harder, to be successful. And finally, they fail to highlight that the path of your career will be filled with setbacks, bumps and bruises and outright failures, and that the game will not always be fair.

Now that we have cleared up what is typically missed, you should know a few more things. Everybody or almost everybody, with the exception of a few lucky or privileged people, begins at an entry level. You'd think that everybody would be aware of this but I have encountered resistance to doing entry level work, when needed, even by individuals who have been in the work force for a few years. Entry levels typically include the most basic, menial, mundane and uninspiring jobs or tasks. They can also mean that you have no authority, are not taken seriously, and are not regarded in the way you would want to be regarded. This is again a cold shower after being the center of attention at your college or university for four years. It can be a rather lonely experience. What's important is to see the big picture and know that there is a light at the end of the tunnel. Some individuals overcome these challenges by grinding in, working as hard as possible, and working very long hours to stand out from the crowd sooner than later. Others find opportunities to relax after work and create more meaningful and soul-nurturing experiences by doing volunteer jobs. Still others have active social lives that allow them to escape the routine and trivialness of their first jobs. There are many options, and you will need to pick what works for you.

After you have found a way to overcome the routine and understand that this is only one period in your career, the next goal is to understand quickly what your employer's expectations are and how to play smart to ensure your advancement. Indeed, the world is open to you but, as I mentioned previously, you have to know what the rules of the game are and how to play that game. Even if you sometimes decide to bend the rules or even not follow them altogether (which might be a bad idea), at least you know what you are dealing with.

One bad mistake I want to share from early in my career is not having a conscious knowledge of any of the above and perhaps not having enough common sense to figure things out quickly. I was in an entry level job that in retrospect was overall a good experience but I worked on a team that was not equipped to integrate and manage early career employees. In addition to being in a job that was filled with unfulfilled promises, which led to a consistent and quick departure of junior staff members, I was once shipped off to do a very low-level administrative job of processing score-card based credit decisions for two weeks. If you have ever done this job, you know what it means – making robotic entries in what is very much a production environment. Throw heavy photocopying duties into the mix and it was a recipe for disaster. I wholeheartedly hated those two weeks, and it was pretty obvious to my supervisors.

One experience to take away from it was the fact that it was only a two-week assignment. While at that time it seemed even more of the same brain-degenerating administrative routine, if not worse, it was just two weeks. My ability to pull through with the highest level of production and a smile on my face could have gone a long away in helping me weather that overall experience, leave a good impression, and work on a plan B to get out of that going-nowhere-job. I did none of that and made an impression I am not happy about even now. Don't forget that everything comes to an end. For the sake of your sanity, find positives in anything you do and work on a back-up plan if you are in not on the right career track.

One final note: despite the boring nature of entry-level jobs, many offer an essential and very fundamental skill set that can prove to be a key to your future success. You can refer to the very early chapters of this book that concluded how number crunching skills are only a small yet crucial part of your success as a credit analyst and a commercial banker. There is no substitute for this experience. If you find this period of your professional life to be uninspiring, you may need to "suck it up." This is the test of endurance. Develop a reputation that you can weather anything and do it with a smile and the most positive attitude. That's what people get hired and promoted for! You cannot force or fake that kind of attitude because people will figure out that you are being disingenuous. Besides, you will hate yourself for not being true to yourself. Look at this as an investment in your own future. Naturally, the best way to "manage" this experience is through finding positive notes and inspiration even in the most trivial and boring tasks. As one of many inspirational readings (but I especially like it when it comes to professional development), consider reading a book called "Fish!" – the story of Seattle's renowned Pike Place fish market. The market is a remarkable example of how you can have a lot of fun doing even the most basic and mundane job. It's all about your attitude!

CHAPTER V – PATIENCE IS SOMETHING THEY JUST DON'T TEACH YOU

Patience and perseverance have a magical effect before which difficulties disappear and obstacles vanish. John Quincy Adams

Here are peculiar attributes assigned to younger generations (your generation!) as compared to more tenured and accomplished generations who are currently in positions of authority and, in some instances, near retirement. We younger generations are often perceived as expecting instant gratification, being entitled, whining, as being unwilling to put in the proper effort yet expecting to be rewarded with professional growth, and impatient. I am using the word "we" for people of my particular generation (born in the 1970s) and now in their 30s, with many of us having already entered or entering positions of authority ranging from middle management levels to even executive levels for the more successful ones. Many of us feel that we are in between the older generations and the younger ones or that we have one foot in each camp. I personally feel that we can relate to both sides, see the strengths and flaws in the views of each camp, and have attributes of both the less and the more tenured generational groups. Of course, these are generalizations and stereotypes, which exist for a good reason – they work within the averages, even if our politically correct society tries to shy away from them.

As a quick clarification, I am referring to "younger" generations as follows (*the generational breakdown was obtained largely from Wikipedia*):

a) Generation Z or Gen Z folks, born in the early 1990s and later; also known as Gen I or Gen Internet or Gen @;

b) Generation Y or Gen Y (loosely defined as people born sometime in the 1980s and through the early 2000s, following Gen X);

c) My generation, or Generation X, is the one in between the "younger" and "older" (born in the late 1960s through early 1980s)

d) I am referring to "older" or "tenured" generations as the Baby Boomers (born 1946-1964; now in their 50s and 60s).

Let's cover why the older generations feel this way about us and what we can learn from in order to improve and be more successful in our careers. Every generation compares its own experiences with what it sees in up and coming generations and expects to see similar qualities. Well, the discovery is that they are not seeing what they would expect to. They grew up in an environment when employee turnover was nearly non-existent, when many people stayed with one employer their entire careers and they would advance one step at a time, after others above them got a chance to move up or retire. There was an implied loyalty both on the part of the employer and employee. It was not a part of professional life to be soul searching all the time for that perfect career track to be happy. Also, the definitions of happiness and balance of work and family life were different and seemingly simpler. Furthermore, the cost of living did not diverge from prevailing salaries. The expectations were different and probably lower when it came to housing, vacations, and many other material things. Debt was not as widely available, people did not borrow as much as possible, and they managed to save.

In summary, workers in my father's generation worked for one organization for their entire career, slowly moved up, often took a lifetime to earn enough for a home that is much smaller than what the expectations are now, took infrequent vacations and certainly nothing fancy like going to the Caribbean on a regular basis, and were content with what they had because that's all they knew. Not to digress but I wonder if that wasn't a simpler way to live. With these standards and expectations came a natural sense of patience. If you were not patient, it was probably a tough environment to be in. Things began to change some time in the 1980s and continued, bringing about the disappearance of both employee and employer loyalty, work becoming more freelance-based, an at-will approach rather than a guarantee of employment, the gap between salaries and the cost of living increasing, especially in urban areas, and finally expectations for the quality of life and for what it meant to be happy on the job changing dramatically. With that, younger and younger generations are being exposed to more and more and, as a result, want to have it all as early as possible. A lifetime of employment to get there is no longer enough. Why wait until you are older to enjoy all the finer things in life, right?

I will reserve my judgment about whether the newer trends are right or wrong. Instead, I want to focus on the differences, as they appear to be perceived. Up and coming generations are less inclined to pay their dues, want to make more and more money as soon as possible, want to grow without necessarily putting in a proper effort, want a balance of work and life right away and do not like to work more than the allotted work week. I see it all around me, including the credit analysis teams I have worked on and managed. Inevitably, you will see the discontent of the older generations. Don't be quick to judge though. Empathy and understanding for why they think as they do is a much better way to handle your differences rather than to feel disenfranchised and get angry about not being understood. Also, do not expect that the other side will do the same, at least not right away. If you do not start with yourself and make it about you, nothing good will ever happen in our world. Think of the quote by Margaret Mead: "A small group of thoughtful people could change the world. Indeed, it's the only thing that ever has."

Ironically, the stark difference between our generations aside, the situation reminds me of the age-old differences between generations of parents and their children. If you look as far back into history as possible, parents have always wanted their children to be like they themselves were and that has never happened. Children have always wanted to follow their own paths and to do things independently and differently from their parents. Disagreements, tensions, and irreconcilable differences are a part of evolution. Apart from the existential issues, now that you may understand why the more tenured generations feel the way they do a bit better, let's focus on how you can use this to your advantage.

First, do not expect them to have the same understanding position; rather, expect that they will be highly annoyed and criticize you (in person or behind your back) for your possible shortcomings. For some reason, I have experienced that those generations are just not good at patiently explaining and teaching their values and expect you to naturally see and embrace them.

Second, recognize that we, just like any generation, have flaws. Everything begins with recognizing that there is a problem and an opportunity to become better. As the next step, you have to have a genuine desire to improve. For example, when I was a junior analyst, I used to have an excessive faith in training and used to downplay practical experience. As I advanced in my career, I grew to appreciate the value of working with a wide range of financing structures, borrowers from a wide range of industries and geographies, a variety of lenders and credit personnel, clients of different financing institutions with different characteristics, and problem loans and economic lifecycles. Some experiences come over a period of time, including changes in attitude.

Three, prove them wrong! Show them that you can put in your time and produce results. Demonstrate that you are not a freeloader and that you are prepared to roll up your sleeves, make the necessary sacrifices, and learn like a sponge. At a minimum, use this as a competitive advantage over your peers because I will assure you that few people consistently and conscientiously work to better themselves and do it in a balanced way.

Four, be patient. Granted, patience is not something that comes easily to younger people who are hungry to achieve and apply their energy to make a difference in the world. I would certainly encourage you not to lose the drive to change the world and make it better. Just recognize that sometimes it will have to happen one step at a time and that is not bad. Yet, this does not mean that you have to spend 20 years reaching the same level of knowledge reached by previous generations. Make sure that your expectations are realistic and sustainable over a longer period of time. As part of your patient approach to a successful career in banking, consider rotations in key business areas such as credit, portfolio management, credit review, lending and business development, training and, finally, management. Understand that it takes a lot of time, money and effort to hire and train an employee, and, while you are learning and growing, think of how you can pay back a company's investment in you. This is why when my team hires even experienced credit analysts, we ask for a 2-3 year commitment to the team. Here is the simple truth – if you do not show commitment and therefore patience, companies will not want to spend time on you!

CHAPTER VI – LEARNING FROM THE BEST – LESSONS FROM A BANKING CEO

On October 27 **the RMA New England Young Professionals' Group** held the CEO Series Event with Paul A. Perrault, President & Chief Executive Officer of Brookline Bank. It was the group's 7th annual event. The goal of this event is to bring together up and coming financial services professionals with some of the most accomplished individuals in the industry, so that younger professionals can learn from their careers, successes and failures.

Mr. Perrault started his career at Shawmut Bank in 1975, spreading financial statements as a credit analyst. He recalled that he never had to look for a job in his career and that opportunities found him. He attributed that to working hard and always being conscious of what was going on in the market-place. During his career he was exposed to various lines of business. One of them was the workout at Old Stone Bank in Providence, RI. Then, an opportunity presented to move to Midwest to work with shared national credits in offering commercial paper backup lines (nobody in the audience seemed to know what that was, given their relatively shorter careers in the industry).

Another career opportunity led Mr. Perrault to New England Merchants National Bank in the late 1970s to develop their wholesale banking business. One experience Mr. Perrault noted is that during those days the goal of a workout was to rehabilitate struggling companies and send them back to the line. This was viewed as evidence of banking success. He also recalled that the reason his bank was competitive was by being a bit kinder, a better bank built on good business practices.

Mr. Perrault talked about the real estate collapse in the Northeast in the early 1990s when the New England market was in a terrible shape. It was around that time that he was pursued by a little bank in Vermont called Chittenden. He spoke fondly of the bank with its community-oriented model. One of the strengths of the bank was the fact that it listened to its customers' needs to develop new products. This is how the bank entered various lines of business including merchant cards and tax-exempt bond financing. After many years of growth, including the acquisition of eight banks, Chittenden was sold in 2007 to People's United Bank.

One of Mr. Perrault's pieces of advice was to move around a bit, in terms of institutions, roles and geography. It is however important to have a supportive spouse or a partner to do this successfully. Another piece of advice is taking opportunities when they come along. Although they may not be what you envisioned or planned for or may not be your perfect opportunity, it is important to recognize them and adjust your plan of action quickly in order to capitalize on them.

During the Q&A session that followed, Mr. Perrault continued to share his personal experiences. He advised the audience to presume that they would be in their job forever, which did not mean being comfortable in what you do and having a sleepy, cushy job. He referred to making it a goal to learn everything you possibly can, doing the best you can, and by doing so that people will notice you. As a manager he always looks for people he can rely on. He recommended being available, ready to roll up sleeves and help, be prepared to raise your hand, and be known for the quality of your work. Also make an effort to learn how organizations are run. Some are run well and some are not. Nonetheless, these are your learning experiences.

When asked about the value of an MBA degree, Mr. Perrault responded that the degree is much more useful for those who do not have a strong business background.

In conclusion, Mr. Perrault answered a question about competing in a highly commoditized banking industry. The key is to keep it simple, price fairly, listen to your customers and stay out of commodities - commodity (mass, low-cost) banking is a dangerous and costly path.

PART V –

GETTING IT DONE IS THE NAME OF THE GAME (PERIOD!)

CHAPTER I – IS YOUR GLASS HALF FULL OR HALF EMPTY?

We all have very positive and very negative people as well as everybody in between surrounding us in our daily lives and in our professional environments. Have you noticed how negative people are a drag on everyone, on their organizations and on themselves personally? I wonder how many of these individuals are aware of their flaws, their true colors and adverse impact on their organizations and colleagues. It is most definitely worse when people have a good idea of their negative qualities and choose to do nothing about them. This is suicidal career arrogance that should not be tolerated by any organization no matter how valued those individuals might be by some executives. Their negativity is the cancer that poisons everything and everyone. Nonetheless, whether by choice or not, nobody wants to deal with sour colleagues.

How negative or positive would you rate your outlook on life (recognizing that even the most positive people have good days and bad days)? The next question is whether your assessment is objective. Here are a couple of tests to help assess your energy levels.

Test #1: Do you thrive on solving challenges or do you fade under their brunt?

Test #2: When you run into a problem, do you consistently come out of each situation with a solution and determination to get the problem addressed or do you have a tendency to complain about the issue, leaving the solution to someone else?

<u>Test #3:</u> Have others rate you anonymously and compare their views with your own assessment. Most commonly, we tend to think of ourselves as better than we actually are. So this is a good test for whether others would agree with your assessment in tests #1 and #2.

A big part of your attitude is how you choose to respond to a problem, very similar to what Charles R. Swindoll spoke of in his quote at the very beginning of this book. Your reaction can vary from annoyance or stress to anger or helplessness, to a smile and a determination to work through the issues. Each one of us always has an option of how to respond to a challenge that life throws at us. One fact is certain: people almost always gravitate toward positive individuals because under the same set of circumstances their positive attitude can be infectious, constructive and something to try to replicate. Our lives are already busy, stressful and at times overwhelming. Who wants to deal with unnecessary negativity?

Using myself as an example, I would be the first one to admit that I was an inherently negative individual. Years ago I could have blamed it on my morbid and hopeless Eastern European upbringing. But that is a very cowardly way of not taking responsibility for who we are. However, my luck changed when at a certain point in my life I began to be surrounded by highly positive individuals for whom every situation was a glass half full rather than a glass half empty. Strangely, and it took months, if not years, my attitude and outlook on life began to change as well. When I began to manage my own team I also noticed that a positive attitude can spread like wildfire. It can disappear just as quickly without consistent presence. Take a look at your team and at other teams around you. You will be surprised to find a correlation in the attitude of team leaders and their teams.

The first step in developing your reputation as a problem-solver is ask yourself how you make things better with every problem. As a credit analyst, you will encounter a range of problems typical of any organization in the industry. Lenders (at least some) view you as an obstacle to getting deals done. They do not want to help you cover all the key analysis points and what's behind the numbers. You are paid much less than your business development peers, while everybody praises the importance and market value of your credit skill. Sales staff can advance very quickly if they deliver, while you may be stuck without a promotion for some time no matter what your accomplishments are in the credit line of business. The list can go on. Each one of these challenges can be dealt with successfully with the right approach. On our credit team we have a rule – do not come up with just a list of problems and complaints. Outline a problem and we can talk. We all need a place to vent and people we can vent to. Beyond venting, however, outline a challenge and come up with one or preferably more ideas on how you can fix it. And, the most important step is actually fixing the issue.

When it comes to hiring, signs of a positive attitude can be more important than any kind of technical expertise to prospective employers – my team and many other organizations look for them. There is a saying that companies hire and fire for attitude, since they can teach technical skills. It is true, with some rare exceptions. Even with those exceptions though, organizations will try to do whatever they can to replace an employee with highly technical knowledge and a rotten attitude with an employee who is more positive. So, unless you are a person with a skill that cannot be replicated, if you want to be successful, being positive and constructive in solving problems is the key in today's world.

A few years ago, I worked with a senior analyst who we will call Tom. For as long as I had been on the team, Tom had an extremely negative influence on his co-workers without even realizing it. It was hardly possible to escape the shadow of his negativity. You would hear his remarks filled with sarcasm and often pure cynicism just about anywhere and every day. Tom was unhappy about a lot of things: lenders did not do their work properly and were responsible for the challenges of his days; the bank did not pay adequately; he was passed on several promotions for unexplained reasons; his credit skills were strong yet no one seemed to acknowledge his expertise; and on and on. These were the more material issues he had; I could spend an entire day recounting lots of trivial issues that endured his scathing commentary.

Although Tom tried to behave himself in the presence of managers and more senior colleagues, his negativity could not be hidden or disguised. During one team meeting, Tom got on his usual high horse complaining about working with a lender who wanted the analysis written in a certain way, which was completely different from how the team was supposed to underwrite and was against the fundamental credit principles. Unfortunately, Tom went ahead with implementing the changes to the analysis that were requested by the lender. To make things worse, it was done without a single discussion with the team leader, without trying to reinforce the proper credit quality and without discussing the challenge with the team leader or asking for his assistance.

When asked by the manager what he did to manage this particular situation to ensure that the credit quality of underwriting was not jeopardized, he became extremely irate and argumentative in front of the entire team. His defense was that he was stuck between lenders and the credit manager, and there was nothing he could do about it. When the manager repeated the question again on what Tom had done to maintain the necessary credit quality, Tom exclaimed that he did nothing. His response was that there was nothing he could do under the circumstances. I suppose nothing other than doing his job, maintaining credit quality, and leaning on the team's manager to support the team's agenda instead of being a mindless note-taker.

Tom kept venting and complaining to the point that the team leader asked him to leave the team meeting – something I have never seen before on any team. While I did not say anything to my team leader, I thought that Tom went overboard. I spoke with a couple of fellow analysts on the team who confessed that they found Tom's tirades to be exhausting and have mentioned to the manager this as a problem. Sadly, as I look back, I could see how we all have been picking up some of Tom's negative energy that was coming through in our attitude toward our work, lenders and the bank.

After our team meeting, Tom and our team leader were behind closed doors for some time, and I am not privy to the details of the details of that conversation. About two to three months later, Tom submitted his resignation letter. There was no announcement, no departure cakes or gatherings and no speeches. Tom was gone without people talking much about him and about why he left. One of my main observations was that after his departure, overall the team's energy picked up, demeanor of several of our team members improved and the working environment became more fun. It is remarkable how one person can have such a noticeable effect on his or her environment. Tom's negativity was part of our daily lives but once he left we all began to breathe more easily.

I would be lying to you if I said that it is easy to be positive. At the risk of offending some of my peers, I'd say that our industry is much more prone to cynicism and negativity than many others. Whether that is because we are exposed to the risks and examples of inappropriate behavior on the part of our borrowers that can ruin our careers if borrowers default on their obligations or because it is the nature of our business to be risk averse and critical, it is hard to say. How do law enforcement, the military, and medical professionals deal with their exposure to the doom and gloom? We can hardly compare banking to those fields. And in many instances they are paid less than we are. There is just no excuse and no place for negativity in your daily lives, if you want to be highly successful as a credit analyst and beyond! Being positive can sometimes make you feel alone but the rewards and opportunities that a positive attitude brings about by far outweigh the risks. This is how people get noticed!

If you think that it is easier to be negative, think of the example of Susan, a very experienced lender I had a chance to work with. It took Susan an inordinate amount of effort to move any deal through underwriting and past approval. There was always someone to blame for that. She would blame the credit managers, the analysts, the overall tightening in the credit culture of the bank, the bank's bureaucracy, her clients, and other factors. Yet she never looked at herself as the problem: she never noticed or admitted how uncooperative and uncollaborative she was, her negative attitude of assuming the worst in people, and her inability to build relationships with credit and non-credit people as the reasons for her failures. To add another twist to the challenge, her main mode of communication was email, which she often used to be nasty and copied everybody under the sun. I heard from senior managers, she was "slotted" to be a lender the rest of her career with little chance for the management track or other advancements. Her days were very difficult, long and always a fight against the prevailing current. If she ever makes a large enough error in her lending decision, her career will be toast as her bosses have no incentive to retain people with his kind of personality. This is no way to work and live.

On the other hand, I worked with an up and coming lender we will call George. While it was not easy to be a junior lender and source deals, he always had a positive attitude and got along with everyone. Since George was not as senior as his colleagues, building bridges and alliances was one skill he had to master. What impressed me about George is that he was always willing and able to extend a helping handing to his junior and senior team members. That helped them manage their respective workflow and showed that George could get the job done when others fail. Colleagues never saw him frustrated or grumpy, and he was genuinely interested in other people, their families, and how he could help them solve their problems. All team members gravitated to him, liked working with him, and went out of their way to help him (with the exception of coworkers like Susan who could not stand George because he embodied their opposite). These are two people in the same organization and the same kind of job, yet they had polar opposite attitudes and polar opposite results which left an imprint on others. One is in a professional graveyard and the other is a banking success story. Which side do you want to be on?

If you ever find yourself running out of steam in being positive, replenish your energy with something that inspires you and shows you that your situation could be much worse. I often go back to two books: the book I mentioned previously – F*ish!* – and a book titled *Pursuit of Happiness*, based on a true story about Chris Gardner. I am certain that all of you have examples that can have this kind of rejuvenating effect. Stay positive!

CHAPTER II – RESULTS ORIENTATION – EFFORT IS GREAT BUT IT DOESN'T LAST FOREVER

First and foremost, in everything you do you need to make an effort, and a good one. This is the most basic element of becoming a successful credit analyst. While the successes of a credit analyst's role are typically hard to translate into numbers (and I would argue that it is a failure on the part of individual institutions to not have a mix of quantitative and qualitative performance measurements), the next step to building a successful reputation is through results you produce. I had an opportunity to work with an analyst who was on a performance improvement plan (i.e. underperforming at that time). This individual was not the smartest or the hardest working person on the team, but I could see that he was genuinely trying to make an effort to do better and to improve. Given that he was making an effort, the management team was willing to give him extra time to correct and improve his performance. Unfortunately though, even in this example, at some point patience ran out because efforts without results can only take you so far in any organization. The level of patience directed at an employee's situation is in part determined by the urgency with which an organization needs to get the job done and generate needed results. Ultimately, every one of us has a finite amount of time after which efforts cease to matter, if they are not converted into the desired achievement.

As you progress in your career, the drive toward results will be more and more important. This is due to the correlation between the growth in rank and increasing focus on the final products of your labor as an organization's way to earn its return on its investment in you. The degree of this emphasis on outcomes will also depend on the economic cycle, your organization's culture, and even the overall social environment of your region and country. All employees and their employers rise and fall by what they do and how they do it. In a capitalist economy such as ours, this focus on results is even more pronounced. You may ask how you as an analyst can be a strong contributor to the bottom line, especially since many organizations measure analysts based on a range of vaguely-defined, elusive qualitative criteria which are subject to managers' interpretation. Even if your organization does not quantify your performance targets, top-performing analysts know there is a set of results-driven criteria that can allow you to rise above your peers. As one of many examples, below is a very brief adaptation of my team's strategic plan that summarizes how an analyst can make his or her own valuable contribution to a commercial bank.

On a high level, a banking organization's single year of financial performance is presented below. Note that this is not an exercise in determining how well a commercial bank operates.

	FY 12/31/xx
Interest Income	$160,000,000
Provisions for Loan Losses	$40,000,000
Net Interest Income / (Loss)	$120,000,000
Fees and Other Income	$130,000,000
Operating Expenses	$210,000,000
Income / (Loss) from Operations	$40,000,000
Income Tax Expense / (Benefits)	$10,800,000
Net Income / (Loss)	$29,200,000

Analysts provide the most valuable direct contributions in three key impact areas, as depicted below:

a) Helping us bring in and close deals by securing approval (net portfolio growth and new income).

b) Making sure that we do not lose money (individual deal level and macro level portfolio management).

c) There is also an often overlooked area: an analyst's ability to help improve income from operations by being more efficient (overhead that produces better results and therefore a better return on a company's investment in its employees) and by identifying ways to save money.

The chart that follows sums up your impact.

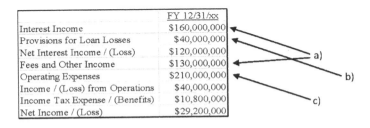

	FY 12/31/xx
Interest Income	$160,000,000
Provisions for Loan Losses	$40,000,000
Net Interest Income / (Loss)	$120,000,000
Fees and Other Income	$130,000,000
Operating Expenses	$210,000,000
Income / (Loss) from Operations	$40,000,000
Income Tax Expense / (Benefits)	$10,800,000
Net Income / (Loss)	$29,200,000

Deals that are booked after analysts underwrite them and help get them approved bring in interest income, fees and other income. Provisions for loan losses is an accounting method of showing how analysts contribute to helping maintain a healthy loan portfolio after loans are booked.

Now, let us dive into more details on key contribution areas.

a) Booking new deals and new income
Generating deals boils down to every analyst's fast turnaround of every deal while maintaining a high level of credit quality. This "production" (outside of scoring worlds) can range from the average of one deal per week to two or even three deals per week, depending on deal/portfolio composition, the extent and complexity of analysis, and the types of deals underwritten. At my peak, I produced on average 2.5 deals per week in a strong credit culture environment with thorough narrative presentation. This is one of several qualities that can make you as an

analyst very attractive as a potential employee! Answer these simple questions:

What is your underwriting turnaround?

Do you do it faster than your peers and what's expected by your organization?

Do you demonstrate continuous improvement in turnaround as you develop and grow as an analyst?

b) Portfolio management

Not losing money means turning over renewals and portfolio reviews fast with a high level of credit quality. This takes place while identifying risks as the lifecycle of a deal and borrower changes and helping make recommendations that lead to changes in credit management strategy to ensure timely repayment.

c) Efficiencies and cost savings

There is a certain cost for every deal, from a pure overhead perspective, from all the people involved in the process, including their salaries, bonuses and benefits. If you take this total annual cost per analyst and divide it by the number of deals each analyst underwrites per year, you will arrive at some form of the cost per deal. Any improvements in the turnaround can lower that cost. It is much tougher to cost out many other duties of an analyst, but not impossible, with underwriting being one of those key responsibilities.

There is a significant impact from earning more income and generating higher interest yields when analysts maintain certain strong and improving levels of deal underwriting turnaround (i.e. incremental improvement). Why focus on the incremental? Every analyst underwrites a certain number of deals. This is just the nature of the job and every job has a production component to it one way or another. It is by going above the average that you make a more meaningful contribution to your institution, thus signaling that you are the candidate to train and grow more aggressively. A potentially negative impact to consider is your inability as an analyst to underwrite deals while balancing a high speed and the quality of underwriting. Lack of such balance can lead to workouts and credit losses. Not underwriting deals fast enough can mean lost revenue and reputation risks to your organization by not getting leads in the future since you could not meet the timelines. If you are the analyst who cannot be relied on for quick turnaround, there is a reputational risk to you personally. You want to be known for being the person to go to for the most complex, largest, and most critical deals – deals that create visibility if done right.

A hidden trove for you as an analyst is to identify ways in which your institution can save money and/or create value besides the efficiencies outlined above. As one example, an analyst on my team identified a new, more efficient industry research service that cost less on an annual basis (annual savings) as well as negotiating a $4,000 annual discount from the list price. The total cost savings was $9,000-$12,000 annually for a better product! This may seem like small money, but we are talking an equivalent of more than 15% in savings equivalent of that analyst's salary. Another example is an analyst who led a focus group to improve various steps of the underwriting process and improve relationships and collaboration with lenders. This effort led to about a 10% improvement in underwriting turnaround that converted to about $50,000 in savings to the bank annually.

The above are very material and in many instances very measurable positive or negative contributions you as an analyst can make. If these are not results, I do not know what is. To conclude the theme of results' orientation, I would like to quote a Chief Credit Officer with whom I had an opportunity to work. This quote very eloquently summarizes what every high performing manager looks for in his or her employee and what can help propel your career: "To me a high caliber employee is the one I can rely on to hand the job to and know that the job will get done and deadlines will be met. I know that this individual will ask for clarifications, if needed, or will ask for guidance. If delays take place or more time is needed, this person will notify me promptly and give me periodic updates if this is a longer duration assignment. This is the person I can count on without hesitation."

I hope that you realize that one way or another every job is results-oriented, whether banking institutions measure those results or not and whether they reward employees for the results or not. Figure out what those results are for you. The most broad and generic are outlined earlier in this chapter: New deals; Portfolio management; and Efficiencies / cost savings. The rest may vary from one organization to another. Not every institution can quantify well what the ROI in your particular line of work is but rest assured that each institution inherently has such ROI. Your number one opportunity is to perform by achieving and exceeding the results that are defined as part of your job. If you are in an organization that does not value results, cannot describe or quantify them, and does not reward them, your opportunity number two is a) to seek clarifications and help create an environment that will be result focused, or b) to look for an organization that values high performance and extend financial and non-financial rewards for a job well-done.

CHAPTER III – WHAT DO YOU WANT TO BE KNOWN FOR AND HOW WILL IT TRANSLATE INTO OPPORTUNITIES?

Your reputation is as good as the last deal you worked on! Every deal matters.

As we head toward the end of this book, you may have noticed that all five elements that will help you build a successful career as an analyst and beyond begin to come together.

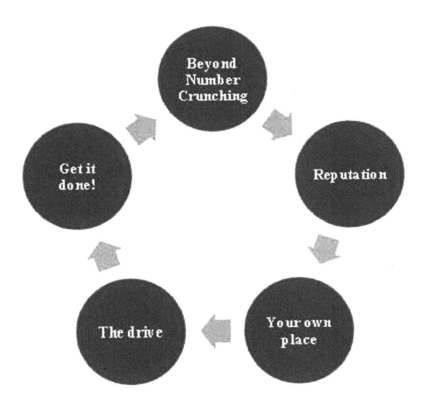

As your reputation as a credit analyst and a financial services professional begins to develop, through your exposure to more individuals within and outside your network people will begin noticing your name. For those who do not have strengths they are known for, people would say that they either do not really know much about you or that they do not have much memorable to note. As you can imagine, more often people will conclude that there is nothing memorable about you, good or bad, or people would have noted it. If you do things right, go above and beyond, accomplish and grow, chances are you will be known for some of these great achievements. The missing component would be to understand what people know or think about you. Do you need to improve the results of your work, the PR message about you in the market, or both?

Let me share a couple of examples. A number of years ago, I began to notice that individuals in my line of duty were somehow familiar with the highlights of my career, my strengths and weaknesses. With a few bankers in my industry my reputation was not good, and these were instances when I might have burned bridges (those bridges were burned for good reasons). However, in the majority of situations, my reputation was quite positive. Once when I was networking with a banking executive and we met to learn more about his business unit, he mentioned that a contact of his thought very highly of me. I was surprised and asked who it was. He provided the name (someone I had met in person only once) and mentioned an XYZ deal that I personally underwrote while I was a lender. This was to help a team member of mine who was a great lender but not as strong on the credit side as I was. It was a club deal with another bank and that lender was a senior lender in charge of the transaction at a bank we agented a portion of exposure to. She commented to my contact that I did a great job underwriting a very large and complex deal with very quick turnaround and that all her bank needed to do was to copy my write-up, because the quality of underwriting was evident.

Besides being pleasantly surprised to have a good reputation, it made me realize that every single deal and every interaction with a prospect, client, network member or even a colleague matters. Some interactions would fall within the "nothing memorable" category, while others stand out as being positive or negative. What you want to make sure is that you put 150% effort into every deal and every assignment. I have heard some people say that they would put in the full effort next time, on the next deal. This never happens. If you live in hopes of tomorrow, you miss out on making a difference today. And guess what, tomorrow there is another tomorrow, and it is vicious cycle.

Your reputation as a credit analyst is as good as your last deal. How did you do on your last deal? And not only what you think but what do others think? Of course, it is true that some great analysts have a fair bit of goodwill built in based on their track-record and achievements. If they stumble, chances are they will get another chance. However, that goodwill is only good for so long and so far. It has an expiration date. People tend to remember bad experiences a lot longer than the good ones, and your challenge is to make sure that you maintain not only a top level of performance but also that you do it consistently.

I recall working with a lender who treated me, other analysts, and many other colleagues like we were nobodies. He would only be nice and polite if he needed you. The rest of the time you were nobody and nothing. Yet, when he was interacting with clients, he was an incredible, personable and high quality business developer and relationship manager. However, because he was unable to build a good working relationship with his colleagues, it was incredibly difficult for him to get his deals underwritten and approved or to resolve problems with his clients that involved others. His standing and reputation within his network made him highly inefficient and quite frankly made his work days very miserable. A fellow lender even noted that this individual had all the personality of a stool! Do you know what you are known for? Don't forget to think of all the people around you, especially your colleagues!

Another example of being known for something is an example of a bank that is no longer around. It was a fast growing institution that was profitable for a number of years, until the economy ran into a wall called the Great Recession (of 2008). As part of the liquidation plan and in order to retain at least some people to burn through the workouts and portfolio liquidations, the bank began handing out titles, ranks and promotions the way snow covers New England during Nor'easters. These employees were happy for a bit. Wouldn't you want to be a Vice President after a couple of years as a credit analyst with barely any experience? Well, when most of these high-ranking individuals began to look for new jobs, the market had a certain stereotype of bankers coming out of this organization. The reputation was that the impressive titles on those resumes meant nothing and that those bankers lacked essential credit and lending experience. While it may not have been the case with everybody (including credit analyst candidates), I have heard through the grape-vine that some institutions were passing on them because of that reputation. This is one of those unfortunate examples of an "unmanaged" reputation that gets out of hand because people talk.

Lastly, to expand a bit on "people talking," we know perfectly well that when it comes to formal reference checks on employees, HR staffers and attorneys will always tell you to provide dry comments that do not disclose anything other than whether or not a person left on good terms and to provide salary verification. Formally, out of fear of law suits, people are tight-lipped. There is, however, a large network of professionals who have worked together at one point or another. This network in my opinion is even closer-knit in banking because there are only so many banks in each region and most of us have worked at the key ones and know each other. There is practically one to two degrees of separation among bankers. Informal exchanges are how a smart prospective employer gets information about you, especially if your reputation is a mystery.

If you think of switching banks as a way to clear your less-than-perfect reputation, there is a pretty good chance that it may not work. Besides, if enough people have had similar challenges with you, it is a good exercise to look at yourself as the root cause of the problem.

One of my team's former analysts has had challenges with receiving and handling feedback. She would very quickly get defensive and argumentative and even snappy with me and other managers. To her credit, by the end of the day she would come in to apologize, recognizing her weakness in handling even constructive criticism. This is what I would call being comfortable in your own skin and being attuned to your weaknesses (it is pretty easy to be attuned to one's strengths). Other than dealing with criticism, this analyst was a strong performer, which motivated me to be patient with her and help her overcome this issue. This is an example of the goodwill built while at work in a team providing a person with the time and resources to become better.

In another, very similar example, an analyst who left my organization a long time ago did not have a good reputation to build on and had issues with criticism. Instead of improving, he focused on blaming the institution and me personally for the issues he had. Remarkably, he consistently used our coaching sessions as an opportunity to provide feedback to me and to outline my "inadequacies" as a manager. He alienated almost everybody he could on the team, including managers, with the only option left – to leave or to eventually be fired. He figured out where things were going and left the organization, in one of the toughest economies and with his colleagues having nothing good to say about him. Although he moved to another region of the country, I can see that it will be difficult for him to secure employment in a very competitive economy when his former colleagues have "no comment" to make about his track-record and reputation in the organization. All of the above are examples of how your reputation can lead to learning, development and growth opportunities, opening new doors for some and permanently shutting them for others.

CHAPTER IV – GET IT DONE AND FIX IT LATER

You will frequently find yourself in situations that make your job extremely difficult. This is true of any organization and any industry, and certainly very common in credit analysis when you have a multi-tier client audience to take care of and please while always working in the best interests of your organization. This balance is a very tough task in itself. However, you can easily turn it into an insurmountable problem if you begin to try to fix the root causes of issues you run into right on the spot. This is a recipe for failure when your focus should be on resolving the immediate challenge at hand. For instance, you may be working on a time-sensitive deal but not getting much cooperation from a lender in helping you address the risks that you know are going to be criticized and will be a poor reflection on the quality of your work as an analyst. What you should be focused on is:

- Asking lots of question to understand the lender's point of view and rationale;

- Explaining to the lender your position from the credit point of view;

- Engaging in an active dialogue to find a resolution;

- Using your persuasive and "soft" influencer skills to help the lender understand what the issues are from the credit point of view;

- Balancing business needs with your bank's credit culture, credit policy guidance and solid knowledge of credit;

- Influencing the lender to do something about the risks in the context of that deal; and

- When warranted, putting your foot down if you need things done in a certain way.

If you engage in the blame game, you will render yourself highly inefficient at completing your primary task. If you try to change the lender, chances are you will gain an "enemy" and will not get the job done. Even if you are 100% correct in trying to change a colleague, people do not change overnight and often do not change 100%, with egos, rank, defensiveness, and many other human flaws getting in the way of working to improve ourselves and our work environment. Thus, keep an eye on the task at hand and GET THE JOB DONE!

As you focus on overcoming immediate challenges, it does not mean that you should forget about the issues that may have created them – not at all. The simple truth is that there is a proper time for everything. Note what the bigger issue is, so that you can try to address it later from the perspective of your position and authority in the organization. The ability to recognize what you can and cannot do on your own to resolve the root cause of a problem will be of incredible value in effecting the desired change. Also recognize that what you perceive to be the issue may not be what the real issue is. For example, you may assume that a lender lacks basic credit skills. While that may be true, over the years I have seen lenders grounded in credit lose track of what is important for the banking business and fall victim of being overburdened with humongous portfolio management responsibilities without proper support, turning into de facto portfolio managers. I have also witnessed how organizations' cultures and compensation plans may divert lenders' attention from managing problems with their existing credits (if it ain't broke, don't fix it, unless it is a workout) in favor of business development. Last but not least, it is possible that your inability to communicate issues effectively is what caused a lender to disregard you. Ultimately, the issue is not always what it might seem! After you note the opportunity for change and complete your immediate task successfully, spend a bit of time to understand the real ailment rather than being misled by the symptoms or the wrong assumptions.

Do not forget that you have to be self-aware and recognize when you are a part of the problem. This quality is in part developed by trying to be objective, fair, self-critical and HUMBLE, no matter what your title is and how much experience and knowledge you have (or you think you have). I recall running a survey of all lenders to determine what our credit team could have done better to support them. Unfortunately, there were some individuals who were baffled by my question of "what they could have done better" and arrogantly noted: "are you kidding?" or "nothing whatsoever." Do not lower yourself to the level of those individuals. Life is about evolution and constantly trying to improve rather than degrade yourself. In order to truly get to the root cause of any challenge in your organization and to successfully resolve it your best ally is compassion and not getting on the bandwagon of blaming others. Stay constructive and focused on the bigger picture and bigger goals.

Here is an example of a lender with whom I have worked for many years (let's call him Dana). He could not stand any kind of process, did not see value in them and would refuse to follow rules, thinking that if he were a good producer, he could do whatever he wanted. The most common example would be getting a package from him to underwrite a deal, and what a painful process it was. Our workflow included a review of the file for completion in order to keep analysts as efficient as possible and focused on the underwriting and turnaround. Dana wanted an analyst to be assigned right away and would want to work with the analyst on any kinds of statement requests and follow up to complete the deal submission. As a team leader I could not let that happen because the team efficiency depended on lenders sending us complete and updated packages. If I did what he asked just to please his personality, I would have been hurting many other lenders the team was serving.

Dana routinely involved his team leader who would come to me on a regular basis to advocate on his behalf, as Dana himself did not want to sit down with me to discuss our relationship and challenges. After several attempts to meet with him to resolve our differences, I gave up trying because I had gone above and beyond without any reciprocal effort. I could never understand why he resisted what seemed to be a reasonable workflow for underwriting. Yet, he would not want to engage in a discussion of how we could do things better while supporting several dozen relationship managers. What made matter worse is the fact that it would take a lot of effort for him just to get his deal placed in the queue for underwriting because of his unwillingness to work as a team. As you can imagine, it took a significant amount of time and effort for him to get his approvals or just to manage his portfolio because his approach was not results-oriented. Rather than getting the job done, he worried about the process, how he disliked it and how to overcome it. Sadly, if there were problems, he did not want to make things better; instead he focused on complaining and fighting the system.

Some of you may ask why you need to think about making changes after you get your immediate job done. Technically, you do not have to. However, if you are a high performer and want to be successful in your career, you should aspire to make a positive impact on your organization by working to address the issues that can make your own and other people's jobs more productive and rewarding. You will find that in our industry in particular, the "if it ain't broke, don't fix it" philosophy is quite prevalent. I am not sure what cause this. Perhaps part of the reason is that we tend to be a reactive and conservative industry, not prone to thinking forward or focusing on constant evolution. Whatever the causes are, I would much rather focus on helping make things better rather than answering existential questions that may not allow me to achieve results and the changes desired.

In conclusion, I want to mention what could be one of the greatest opportunities in our industry. Banking and commercial banking specifically has not changed in a long time – in fact, the more it changed, the more it stayed the same. While the core of our business has been the same for centuries – take deposits, use this money to make good loans, and collect the money in a timely manner to repeat the cycle over and over – there is an incredible variety of business models, cost structures, combinations of products and services and human capital qualities. What has been lacking in general is a focus on solving the problems that plague us. We as an industry have not been focused on being creative, innovative and entrepreneurial while keeping credit quality at the core of our business. If you are a credit analyst who can be innovative and creative and if you can align the forces around you as a real entrepreneur to get things done, you will be an invaluable member of any banking team. Granted, that path will not be easy because you will almost always be sailing against the current. However, for those who can overcome the barriers, the rewards can substantially outweigh the risks and challenges.

CHAPTER V – NO ONE CARES ABOUT WHAT YOU WANT, UNLESS …

I would like to wrap up the main content of this book with a very simple truth that many of us often forget – no one cares about you and what you want until you care about what's important to others. Call it selfish human nature, the impersonal world we live in, survival of the fittest, or a lack of emphasis on certain human values that our society does not hold in high regard. Whatever the underlying reasons are, by focusing on what is important to others you can achieve your own goals, learn, develop, grow and have a satisfying career as well as work-life balance.

There is a concept known as "common currency." I first learned about this concept when I was working on my MBA at Babson College; read more in the work by Babson professor Allan Cohen and Stanford professor David Bradford. It is an influence model to influence other people by first focusing on what is important to them. It is a process of reciprocity and exchange that can and should be used effectively in business as well as in personal settings. A part of the challenge and therefore an opportunity is to learn what is important to others and why. "You get what you give" is one of the implications of this methodology, which masterfully verbalizes and conceptualizes what some successful people have taken advantage of to drive their success for generations.

Think about what is important to commercial lenders, as they are your first-line customer. Chances are the list would include the following:

- Getting loans approved and closed;

- Getting the above done quickly and efficiently;

- Sifting through a list of prospective deals and focusing on the ones that are more likely to happen;

- Understanding key risks quickly and efficiently to structure as few covenants as possible to minimize the greatest risks;

- Booking as many deals as possible and growing the portfolio;

- Booking the highest interest rate and fee income loans in this very competitive environment;

- Getting back to clients as quickly as possible with their daily issues addressed in a way that will bring about the highest level of satisfaction possible;

- Managing their portfolios to ensure a high level of quality and flagging and addressing problems as early in the process as possible.

The next task is to build a list similar to the one above of what is important to your manager, your colleagues, credit departments in general, the bank's clients and, finally, the bank proper. You may want to think about the shareholders or the various stakeholders of your institution because we all work to bring value to them as well. While this deals with a very detailed picture of how and why a banking organization exists, such a view is important when you are early in your career to keep you motivated, encourage you to do better, help you see the forest and the trees, and remind you that there is a light at the end of the tunnel even for lowest level jobs.

Now make a list of what you can do to help lenders and other "constituents" of yours to achieve their goals. This is perhaps the highest level of customer service and every job has that orientation, whether people realize it or not. If you recognize this, you will be able to build a formidable brand for yourself by delivering high value to members of your network, within your organization and beyond. This is why when you get a call from someone who needs your assistance, your first question should be "how can I help?"

It happens at times that in order to learn as much as possible, to develop as a credit analyst from technical and non-technical perspectives, and grow, you may need to move around, whether it is in different roles within one organization or other organizations that fit your career goals and provide the challenges you seek. Nonetheless, it is by focusing on other people's common currency that you should be able to deliver high quality results, make your colleagues' and clients' lives easier, and build the goodwill that will help you grow.

CHAPTER VI – LEARNING FROM THE BEST – LESSONS FROM A BANKING CEO

On November 16 the RMA New England Chapter held its 6th Annual CEO Series Event featuring Kevin Bottomley, CEO of Danversbank. The event was organized by the Chapter's Young Professionals Group. It was born from an idea the most experienced and distinguished bankers in Massachusetts and new generations of banking professionals face-to-face. Past events have featured CEOs and Presidents of Boston Private, Citizens Bank, Eastern Bank, Cambridge Trust and Wainwright Bank.

Mr. Bottomley shared with the attendees a number of his career experiences. The highlights included understanding that aligning yourself with specific senior executives can be a double-edged sword. On the one hand you may have a good mentor. On the other, an alignment that is too close can lead to your falling out of favor, if your mentor steps down. Overall, Mr. Bottomley underscored the importance of having good mentors. He also advised exploring various lines of business as specializing too early in one's career can restrict longer term growth.

In the realm of lessons learned, Mr. Bottomley shared an experience at one of his past employers. The bank engaged in construction projects that were a credit policy exception. The institution ran into trouble after doing more of these deals than it should have. The conclusion is that the credit policy is there for a reason. Too much of a good thing resulted in significant losses as lending became unreasonable.

One of Mr. Bottomley's most valuable experiences as a senior manager was to hire the right people and get out of their way. Some of his first hires as a CEO were individuals who were easy-going, smart, and had a great work ethic. Mr. Bottomley is also a firm believer in constant learning. To this day his bank has a program that puts new-hires in front of HR after six months of employment to learn about their past experiences and what the bank could be doing better / differently. His personal style is not to overanalyze things. Good managers are people who can operate on incomplete information, make decisions, live with them, are quick to understand when something doesn't work, and can fix the problem in a timely manner. Mr. Bottomley learned over the years that a senior manger cannot make all decisions. He believes in not "shooting down" people if they make mistakes, and in using those mistakes as learning opportunities. He sees it as part of his job to make people better. His mantra is to work hard but also to have fun in the process.

Throughout the presentation and during the Q&A, Mr. Bottomley talked about learning constantly, learning as much as possible, and not being afraid of challenges. He also suggested to the attendees to find out how their organizations make money to help guide them in selecting career tracks. Another suggestion was to network outside of banking. Last but not least, if you want fast-growth careers, you should look for organizations with a growth track-record that is reflected by growth in assets, loan portfolios, and P&L trends.

THE PREVIEW FOR CREDIT ANALYSIS 103

You know nothing

If you are on track to developing Credit Analysis 102 qualities, you should not forget that your evolution as a person and a professional is a never-ending endeavor. Now may be a good time to lay the foundation for future growth or Credit analysis 103 skills. In order to help you with this next challenge, here are a few next level qualities to work on.

What do you think is the number one cause of the career demise of bankers (as well as non-bankers)? You are correct if you pick arrogance as the culprit. Arrogance stems in part from being around long enough and seeing enough to begin developing a sense that you know it all. The remarkable irony is that the same people who develop it probably used to detest the arrogant, tenured bankers they encountered earlier in their careers, who thought they knew it all and treated them, as rookies, without basic respect and dignity. Unfortunately, we often risk turning into something we have despised. The common excuse is "our environment has shaped us this way over time." Do not let the environment shape you – shape your environment! As this book was being finalized, I attended an event organized by the RMA New England Chapter titled "Booking prudent loans in uncertain times; applying lessons learned to avoid past mistakes." The Moderator, David Aloise, offered a quote that fits well here: "It's a person's ignorance that gets them into trouble and their arrogance that keeps them there."

Your goal should be working effectively with individuals of different ages, different experience levels, and different titles. The key to doing it successfully is by assuming that "you know nothing"! I am not implying that you should pretend to be dumb. Not at all. Your knowledge and expertise is something you will always have. What I am proposing is understanding that you will always continue to learn and that this process continues 24/7, 365 days a year, for the rest of your lifetime. This attitude will also help you to never stop learning, developing and growing. Smart people know that they can learn from their peers, their seniors, and even their juniors. The same highly intelligent people also learn constantly not only from their industry, but also from industries that have nothing to do with the world of financial services or finance, and some examples can come easily from the surrounding environment, similar to how this book was inspired (but more on this some other time).

Humble learning and the cancer that crushed it

It has been noted time and time again that our risk-averse industry has produced lots of cynics over the years. Place safeguards within you to build in essence a Great Wall of China between your persona and anything within our industry that may be perceived as negative. Being humble and reinforcing that quality is what allowed people to preserve the good they had while they climbed the corporate ladder of success. Recognize that cynicism and even sarcasm in the workforce and in your personal lives is the cancer that will eventually poison your every cell and spread to people around you. It may be funny to observe cynical comedians on stage and have a healthy laugh with your friends, but don't bring that negativity into your work and life.

The most revealing truth is that we cannot control the inception of cancer that can occur within our physical bodies, but the "cancer" in our attitudes is 100% preventable and within our control. Yet, it is a choice that you will make between staying humble or choosing the path of arrogant self-destruction that will sooner or later catch up with you and the environment and people that surround you.

What makes up an excellent credit analyst?

As part of writing this book, I thought that it would be relevant to ask some of our colleagues "what it means to be an excellent credit analyst." Some of the first reactions I received in response can be summarized as, "what a loaded question!"

The profile of 23 respondents ranged from credit analysts to chief credit officers. With the exception of one, all were or still are credit analysts, which tells me that these individuals have firsthand experience in being and/or managing credit analysts. The pool of respondents has a whopping combined 180 years of work as credit analysts, which equates at the very least to 9 years of work experience each as credit professionals.

The key goal of this small (non-scientific) research endeavor was to identify up to ten qualities that make up an outstanding credit analyst. There were 166 qualities cited, a number of which clearly overlapped.

The majority of key skills that go into building a high class credit analyst were non-quantitative in nature. This is not surprising because we are talking about a profile of a well-rounded analyst. Number crunching and technical aspects are the very foundation of credit training, as noted earlier in the book. As you progress further, you will not become a quality analyst if you lack the quantitative, accounting, and other technical skills that are necessary. However, to ensure your further and longer term growth, many non-quantitative talents become more relevant and will be at the forefront of your successes. The top five, most frequently noted qualities were (in frequency only, not in the order of perceived importance):

- Detail-oriented;

- Analytical in nature;

- Communication skills;

- Time management skills; and

- Writing skills.

A few other qualities mentioned in their order of declining frequency:

- Accounting and financial statement analysis experience;

- Interpersonal skills;

- Organizational skills and multitasking skills; and

- Credit / banking experience.

As we focus on the top skills outlined by the respondents, "attention to details" and "analytical in nature" were mentioned as the top quality by five of the 23 as the number one quality! Accounting knowledge took the third spot. If we look at the qualities among the top three most frequently named by the respondents, you will find "analytical in nature" or having analytical skills at the top with seven votes. "Detail-oriented" and "knowledge of accounting" shared the second place with six votes. They were followed closely by "communication skills" and "writing skills" with five and four votes, respectively.

To recap, the mostly frequently mentioned five top qualities are:

- Analytical skills

- Detail-oriented and accounting skills

- Communication skills

- Writing skills

It should also be noted that qualities such as communication and interpersonal skills have a lot in common.

What does all this mean to you? This survey largely supports a number of the conclusions already made in this book. It also points out what experienced colleagues and managers value and look for in high performing (and possibly non-high performing) credit analysts. I would also recommend that you evaluate yourself objectively on how you would rank in these qualities.

I wish you the utmost success in your career as a credit analyst and hope that this book will be of help!

AFTERWORD

As I was undertaking the writing of this book, without nearly as much inspiration as I would have liked, the announcement of the death of Steve Jobs came in. I was never a huge fan of Mac or Apple, other than having them everywhere in college and liking them for the lack of other options. Well, not exactly liking as they were constantly crashing back then as I recall. That snafu aside, my knowledge of Steve was limited to just knowing the fact that he was the CEO of Apple, a few Apple-related cases in business school, and the reference to Apple in Forest Gump. However, as the news of his death spread, I began to realize that the man was an inspiration for a number of innovations that reshaped how we think and the way we do things. As my wife commented, the death of very few people on Earth would have led to as much sympathy and sadness as did Steve's death.

The day after his death, Steve Jobs' Stanford address was all over the Internet, and I picked a link from a friend's post on Facebook. I watched it. And then it hit me... the renewed inspiration for completing this book and making it an honest, valuable, hopefully even an inspiring resource to my audience. There were a lot of words said that could inspire even the most uninspired of us. However, Steve Jobs' speech stands out in particular: "Your time is limited, so don't waste it living someone else's life. Don't be trapped by dogma, which is living with the results of other people's thinking. Don't let the noise of others' opinions drown out your own inner voice, heart and intuition. They somehow already know what you truly want to become. Everything else is secondary."

We are so caught up in our daily rat race that we become less and less inspired as we grow older (or younger for some us). Do not lose that spunk and idealism we all have in our earlier year. Do not lose your true self under the weight of needing to pay your mortgage and being buried under deadlines. And who would have thought that the day of a man's death would be the inspiration I so needed. Well, my time is limited too....